THE PROBLEM-PLAY

AND ITS INFLUENCE ON MODERN THOUGHT AND LIFE

BY

RAMSDEN BALMFORTH

HASKELL HOUSE PUBLISHERS Ltd.
Publishers of Scarce Scholarly Books
Brooklyn, NY
1977

HASKELL HOUSE PUBLISHERS LTD.
Publishers of Scarce Scholarly Books
Brooklyn, NY

Library of Congress Cataloging in Publication Data

Balmforth, Ramsden.
    The problem-play and its influence on modern
thought and life.

    Reprint of the 1928 ed. published by G. Allen
& Unwin, London.
    1. Drama—History and criticism. 2. Theater—
Moral and religious aspects. I. Title.
PN1647.B32 1977   809'.933'5   76-52915
ISBN 0-8383-2129-2

Printed in the United States of America

PREFACE

THE purpose of this book is to show how deeply Problem-Plays have influenced, and may influence, the public mind not only on sex and marriage problems, but also on social, ethical, and religious problems. It may serve also, I hope, as an introduction to a more serious study of the drama in our schools, colleges, and dramatic societies and institutions, and thereby help in raising the standard of public taste and the type of drama which is presented in our theatres. We ought not to rest satisfied until the standard of taste and appreciation in dramatic art reaches the level of that of the ancient Greeks—though we are a long way from that at present.

One or two of the Reviewers of my previous book, *The Ethical and Religious Value of the Drama*, complained that in that work I had not paid sufficient attention to the drama as an art. But the title of the book should have warned them not to expect that. In the following pages, however, I have devoted an introductory chapter to the relation of ethics to art, and especially to the art of the drama. I have let the dramatists speak for themselves, and I have shown, briefly, that philosophic thought supports their claim—the claim, that is, that the drama is something more than an appeal to the senses, or a mere means to pleasure. At its best, it is, as Viscount Morley says of poetry, " a means of bringing the infinite into our common life," giving us " quietness, strength, steadfastness, and purpose, whether to do or to endure. All art or poetry that has the effect of breathing into men's hearts, even if it be only for a space, these moods of settled peace, and strongly confirming their judgment and their will for good, is great art and noble poetry."

This is not to say that poetry and dramatic art are to be judged solely by ethics, but it does mean that art, seeking after perfect expression in the material which the artist selects, must give us " more abundant life," or it fails in its purpose. And in that more abundant life, and the impression it makes and the influence it has on the inner spirit, ethics, or our conception of ethical values, helps us in our judgment upon any work of art, dramatic or other.

With this principle in mind, the reader will see how, from the earliest ages, the best drama has helped to purify the soul, not only, as in tragedy, " by pity and by fear," but also by " admiration, hope, and love." And especially, as I have shown in the following pages, has it helped to purify religious customs and ideas from cruel and superstitious elements, and to give to men a truer conception of their relation to each other, and to those unseen spiritual laws and forces which guide the universe, and create and condition our life.

R. B.

CONTENTS

The testimony of the Dramatists themselves. Art for
Life's sake. The ethical qualities necessary for the creation
of a work of art. The difference between artistic ability
and artistic appreciation. Ruskin on the relation of art
to ethics. The aim of both—to develop a finer personality.
The testimony of Plato in the *Symposium*.

CHAPTER II

Ibsen's influence. Tolstoy's *The Light Shines in Darkness*.
Bernard Shaw's *Major Barbara*. Galsworthy's *Strife* and
The Skin Game. The ethical problem stated precisely by
Ibsen, Tolstoy, and Shaw.

CHAPTER III

The question complicated by the economic dependence of
woman. St. John Ervine's *Jane Clegg*. Stanley Hough-
ton's *Hindle Wakes*. Miles Malleson's *The Fanatics*.
Ibsen's *When We Dead Awaken*. The mystery of sex.
The danger of generalizations. Shakespeare's, Ibsen's,
Shaw's, and Meredith's women. Edward Carpenter's *The
Intermediate Sex*. The necessity for Restraint—and Charity.

THE PROBLEM-PLAY

CHAPTER I

DRAMATIC ART IN ITS RELATION TO ETHICS

THE Drama, and especially Tragedy, says Thomas Hill
Green, " implies a conscious effort of the spirit, made
for its own sake, to recreate human life according to
spiritual laws." This saying of the philosopher is borne
out by the poets and the dramatists themselves. " The
highest moral purpose aimed at in the highest species
of drama," says Shelley, in his introduction to *The Cenci*,
" is the teaching the human heart, through its sympathies
and antipathies, the knowledge of itself ; in proportion
to the possession of which knowledge every human
being is wise, just, sincere, tolerant, and kind." " Every
grouping of life and character," says John Galsworthy
to the same effect, " has its inherent moral ; the business of the dramatist is so to pose the groups as to
bring the moral issue poignantly to the light of day."
" Dramatic art," says Mr. Granville Barker, " is the
working out—not of the self-realization of the individual,
but of society itself. A play is a pictured struggle and
reconciliation of human wills and ideas ; internecine,
with destiny or with circumstance. The struggle must
be there, and either the reconciliation, or the tragedy of

the failure, and it is generally in the development of character by clash and mutual adjustment that the determinant to the struggle is found. What livelier microcosm of human society, therefore, can there be than an acted play ? . . . Neither topically, nor in terms of direct reason, nor of pure faith, but by the subtler way of art the drama works, to evolve from the sentient mass a finer mind, responding to the fine fellow-mind of the poet—expressed in terms of a common experience through the medium of human beings—whose art has that deeper significance that we find in the faces and voices of friends with whom we have come through the gates of understanding." And finally I may quote Bernard Shaw to the same effect : " I am convinced that fine art is the subtlest, the most seductive, the most effective means of propagandism in the world, excepting only the example of personal conduct, and I waive even this exception in favour of the art of the stage, because it works by exhibiting examples of personal conduct made intelligible and moving to crowds of unobservant, unreflecting people to whom real life means nothing."

If the reader will call to mind the great dramas of the world he will realize how wide has been their appeal, and how they have helped to change and develop human thought, ethics, and religion. Knowledge of one's self, moral issues, the mystery of Personality and of Destiny, the ways of God to man, education into new truth, new ideas, and great causes—these are the justification of the problem-play and the claim of the dramatist " to recreate human life according to spiritual laws."

There are some people who say that they do not like problem-plays. When they go to the theatre they go to spend a pleasant hour, to be interested, or amused. Amusement and pleasurable interest have, of course, their place in art and in life. But to regard them as the aim and purpose of art is like regarding the candles and vestments, or the music and symbols of the ritualist as the aim and purpose of religion. I think it was Carlyle who satirized this attitude of mind as the pot-house attitude, and the art which sets itself to pander to it as pot-house art. As a matter of fact, every great play is a problem-play. Just as behind every comedy there is tragedy lurking somewhere near, so every serious play ends with a note of interrogation. What was the secret defect in Hamlet's character? What was the measure of Lady Macbeth's guilt, not only as against Duncan, but against Macbeth? Had Othello some inherent failing in his personality which made him merely as dough in the unscrupulous hands of Iago? Was not King Lear's querulous vanity too cruelly punished? And how, from the standpoint of Eternal Justice, shall we justify the sacrifice of Cordelia? Was the feud between the Montagues and the Capulets the destined cause of the tragic fate of Romeo and Juliet? Were the intrigues, and hatreds, and ambitions of the Wars of the Roses the cause of the numerous tragedies in *Richard III*? And what was the overpowering mystery underlying the terrible personalities of Iago,

Richard III (as described by Shakespeare), and Francesco Cenci ? Such questions are endless. Every serious play is a problem-play.

The great dramatist, like the great poet, is in some sense a prophet. He foresees the movement of ideas, thoughts, feelings, sympathies, and antipathies, which are slowly moving the hidden forces of life. He portrays these on the stage, and, in so far as he is in advance of his generation, he meets the fate of all prophets—insult, derision, poverty, social ostracism, and other modern substitutes for imprisonment and martyrdom. Bernard Shaw, in his *Quintessence of Ibsenism*, has collected a few of the gems of virulent criticism and invective with which Ibsen's plays were greeted when they were first staged in England. But Ibsen, Tolstoy, Shaw, Galsworthy, Granville Barker, and others of the same school, have long since come into their own. The problem-play, the discussion play, has won as secure a place for itself as the music-drama of Wagner in a somewhat different field. It demands, of course, just as science and religion are demanding, a higher quality of intelligence. With all its shortcomings, the theatre-going public of to-day is more intelligent, more intellectually alert, more critical, than the theatre-going public of the days of Victorian melodrama. Long before the war the new drama had begun to drive out the old, just as the new prophetic thought of Carlyle, Ruskin, Matthew Arnold, and William Morris, in other fields, had prepared the way for new ethical ideals and responsibilities. Ibsen, Tolstoy, Hauptmann, Shaw, and

Galsworthy carried the new spirit into the theatre, and their prophetic delineations of the personalities of the then rising or coming generation, and the type of society and civilization which would arise through such personalities, were pregnant with both hopes and forebodings. But Life, like a lame dog, comes limping after Thought, and the developments which led to the problem-drama were arrested by the Great War. Society, in so far as it was not engaged in war-work, reeled back for a time, by sheer reaction, to the " pot-house " forms of art, and the movement of thought of which the problem-drama was the outcome, was stayed for a time by the great *débâcle*. The war, as everyone now sees, was the culmination of an epoch, and after it was over, the development and study of the drama, and particularly of the problem and discussion-play, proceeded apace. We see signs of this everywhere in the numerous Dramatic Societies, Drama Leagues, Repertory Theatres, the Little Theatre movement, and the widespread study of the drama in schools, colleges, and even in some churches.

Several critics of my book on *The Ethical and Religious Value of the Drama* complained that I had not approached the subject from the point of view of dramatic art. But the very title of my book should have warned them that I had strictly limited myself to the ethical significance and interpretation of the drama. I leave the treatment of the artistic and æsthetic side to those who are more familiar with that aspect of the subject, and who can speak with more authority than I can upon it. But it may be as well here to point out the difference between the two aspects, and to show why the ethical side should be constantly present to our minds. As a matter of fact, I do not think the two aspects can be definitely or permanently separated from each other. Both have their separate appeals to different types of mind, and both have their respective values, but to me the ethical value is the higher. The maxim " Art for Art's sake " must be subordinated to the maxim "Art for Life's sake," just as the greater must include the less. These great words—Art, Life, Truth, Beauty, Good, have an infinite meaning. They are difficult to define with precision, and if we use them interchangeably and substitute our own preconceptions of them—with our varying individual emphasis, bias, or idiosyncrasy— for the infinite for which they stand, we only introduce confusion into our thought. Truth, Beauty, Good— these are the three aspects of the infinite which correspond to the Intellect, the Feelings, and the Will. Surely it is obvious that these cannot be separated from each other. They are indissolubly bound together—the feelings react upon the mind, the mind upon the will, the will again upon the feelings, and the mind, in its judgments, upon both. We cannot cut Life, or the human soul, into segments. Each part or aspect has an active influence on the other, art upon ethics, both ethics and art upon our value-judgments, our value-judgments upon the Will—the end and aim of all being Life, more abundant life.

Or—to put the matter in another way—just as, in the sphere of the intellect, there are right and true ideas, and wrong or false ideas, so, in the sphere of feeling, there are right and true feelings and emotions, and wrong and base feelings and emotions—the right and true feeling of the mother for her child, the false and base feeling of the miser for his gold. And this work of discrimination between right, healthy, and true feelings and emotions, and wrong, false, and base feelings and emotions is always being thrown back upon us, upon our intellectual and moral judgments. And though it may be said that " Beauty is in the eye of the beholder," or, more truly, that the mind behind the eye of the beholder conditions and limits his perception of Beauty, there is always a capacity for growth and development in the appreciation of the beautiful—steps by which the soul mounts upward, as Plato says. But this growth and development of the faculty of artistic appreciation must proceed along with the growth and development of other sides of our nature. The uncultured man may be satisfied for a time with the jingle and jazz of the music-hall, but ere he can appreciate or enjoy the music of Mozart or Beethoven he will have to pass through a long course of education not only in the sphere of feeling and the appreciation of music, but also in the sphere of the intellect, with all its reactions on his ethical and emotional nature.

The truth I am trying to emphasize will be seen still more clearly if we call to mind the ethical qualities which are necessary to the creation of any great work of art. Take a few of these, such as the capacity for hard and sustained work, restraint or self-control, reverence, and humility. All these are indispensable conditions of entry to the Temple of Art, indispensable also to any really creative or executive skill and power.

First, hard work for love of the thing you are shaping. The old Anglo-Saxon meaning of the word worship is significant in this connection. Worship—*weorthscipe*— that is, the ideal worshipped is *worth-shaping* into a thing of beauty, and such work, such worth-shaping, has a definite ethical influence on life.

Second, Restraint or Self-control. That is, not merely the *exercise* of artistic power, but the restraint which the artist imposes on himself, both in his period of training and in the exercise of his art, until he acquires such self-control and self-mastery that his powers seem to come not by *effort*, but by sheer ease and grace of natural skill.

Third, Reverence. Reverence, not only for the natural beauties by which we are surrounded, the beauties of sea and earth, of sky and flower, or the beauty and the mystery of a child's heart, but reverence also for the world of beauty which the great artist is striving to unveil or reveal to the wondering eyes of men so that he may say to them : " Come unto me and see the treasure that I have wrought, discovered, or revealed, for it will bring you rest, surcease from care, and peace of soul."

Fourth, Humility. Humility ! that we poor mortals, with our little minds—" shallow cups " as Oscar Wilde called them—should think to envisage, or comprehend the infinite beauties of this wonderful universe, with all its deep outer mysteries of energy, colour, form, and sound, and its deeper inner mysteries of consciousness, passion, tenderness, mercy, love, and inward peace.

It is true indeed that the opposites of these qualities may be found in the same personality. Along with capacity for hard work in one direction there may be much carelessness and laziness in other directions. Along with restraint and self-control in one thing, there may be unbounded passion and self-abandonment in others. Along with reverence there may be irreverence ; along with humility there may be arrogance and egoism. I need only refer the reader to Oscar Wilde's *De Profundis*, or to the life of Benvenuto Cellini for illustrations. All which seems to imply that Life itself is an art, a poise or balance of feeling, intellect, and will, or, as Aristotle would say, " the observance of the mean." But how is this golden mean possible in a world of struggle, conflict, and tragedy, which demands deep feeling, heroic temper, and resolute will ? For to do the right things " to the right person, to the right extent, at the right time, with the right object, and in the right manner, is by no means easy ; and that is the reason why right doing is rare and praiseworthy and noble." [1] Truly, he who can do these things is the supreme artist.

It may be objected that though these ethical qualities —capacity for work, self-restraint, reverence, and humility—are necessary to the artist in the exercise of his creative powers, they are not necessary to the æsthetic

[1] *Nicomachean Ethics*, Book II, 9, 2.

enjoyment of the spectator in the pleasure which he derives from the contemplation or the study of a work of art. Ruskin has answered this objection so completely and effectively that I need only quote his words. It is the fashion nowadays in some quarters to deride Ruskin, but in his ethics, economics, and æsthetics he was, I believe (with certain reservations), essentially and profoundly right. On the particular matter with which I am now dealing he speaks, it seems to me, with the authority of a Master.

" All great Art," he says, " is the work of the whole living creature, body and soul, and chiefly of the soul. But it is not only *the work* of. the whole creature, it likewise *addresses* the whole creature. That in which the perfect being speaks, must also have the perfect being to listen. I am not to spend my utmost spirit and give all my strength and life to my work, while you, spectator or hearer, will give me only the attention of half your soul. . . . All your faculties, all that is in you of greatest and best, must be awake in you, or I have no reward. The painter is not to cast the entire treasure of his human nature into his labour merely to please a part of the beholder ; not merely to delight his senses, not merely to amuse his fancy, not merely to beguile him into emotion, not merely to lead him into thought ; but to do *all* this. Senses, fancy, feeling, reason, the whole of the beholding spirit, must be stilled in attention or stirred with delight ; else the labouring spirit has not done its work well. For observe, it is not merely its *right* to be thus met, face to face, heart to heart ; but it is its *duty* to evoke this answering of the other soul : its trumpet call must be so clear, that though the challenge may by dullness or indolence be unanswered, there shall be no error as to the meaning of the appeal ; there must

be a summons in the work, which it shall be our own fault
if we do not obey. We require this of it, we beseech this of
it. Most men do not know what is in them till they receive
this summons from their fellows : their hearts die within
them ; sleep settles upon them, the lethargy of the world's
miasmata ; there is nothing for which they are so thankful
as that cry, ' Awake, thou that sleepest.' And this cry must
be most loudly uttered to their noblest faculties ; first of all,
to the imagination, for that is the most tender, and the soonest
struck into numbness by this poisoned air ; so that one of
the main functions of art, in its service to man, is to rouse
the imagination from its palsy, like the angel troubling the
Bethesda pool ; and the art which does not do this is false
to its duty, and degraded in its nature. It is not enough that
it be well imagined, it must task the beholder also to imagine
well ; and this so imperatively, that if he does not choose to
rouse himself to meet the work, he shall not taste it, nor
enjoy it in any wise." (*Stones of Venice*, vol. iii, chapter iv,
sec. xxi.)

Despite all this, however, there is a very natural and
an almost instinctive objection in many minds to any
form of art which seeks to convert people to a particular
point of view. It is expressed in the common saying :
" We don't want to go to the theatre, the concert hall,
the picture gallery, or the cinema, to be made ' good.' "
And obviously there is a point at which didacticism and
propagandism may be used in art for partisan, sectarian,
and even for selfish and pernicious purposes. I read,
for example, of certain business firms in America making
use of the drama for advertising purposes—which opens
up a somewhat frightful prospect. But we have to take
the risk of these things just as we have to take the risk
of steamships being turned into ironclads, or aeroplanes

into droppers of bombs and chemicals. If art is turned
to base or selfish uses, that is no more the fault of art
than it is the fault of religion that it is sometimes made
a cloak for hypocrisy or an incentive to hatred and
persecution ; or the fault of science that its beneficent
discoveries are turned to purposes of evil and its
instruments to means of terror and destruction. After
all, we come back to the saying of Keats, that the
purpose of life and experience, with all its sorrows and
sufferings, is to create or develop more intelligent souls.
And if this is the purpose of Life, it is the purpose of
Art, and indeed of Religion and Science also—to create
more intelligent souls, that is, to enable us to pierce
more deeply into the *reality* of things. And surely this
is a " good," though in a different and larger sense from
that in which the word is customarily used. It ought,
therefore, to be possible so to define the relationship
between art and ethics as to show their intimate and
indissoluble spiritual connection, their common aim and
purpose. And I venture to state that relationship in
this way :

That the common aim of art and ethics is, first, to
develop a deeper and finer personality ; in other words,
to give us more abundant life. Second, that the
opportunity for the development of personality through
art, science, and educational and social institutions
should be freely open to all, that everyone may have the
opportunity of so training all his faculties and powers
that he may use them at their very best. That is, the
appeal of art is a universal appeal. Third, that in this

development of personality towards a higher culture and a higher way of life, we must carry our brothers along with us in our march towards the " plains of Heaven." Not in contemplation alone, not in æstheticism alone, can we find the highest way of life. Or, as Matthew Arnold so truly says : " Not a having and a resting, but a growing and a becoming, is the character of perfection as culture conceives it. And because men are members of one great whole, and the sympathy which is in human nature will not allow one member to be indifferent to the rest, the expansion of our humanity, to suit the idea of perfection which culture forms, must be a general expansion. . . . The individual is required, under pain of being stunted and enfeebled in his development if he disobeys, to carry others along with him in his march towards perfection, to be continually doing all he can to enlarge and increase the volume of the human stream sweeping thitherward."

It is in this sense that some of our greatest poets and dramatists have spoken of themselves as teachers ; that Bernard Shaw speaks of dramatic art as " the subtlest, the most seductive, the most effective means of propagandism in the world " ; that Wagner invited his readers to come to his music-drama as to a religious service ; and that Plato, in that famous passage in the *Symposium*, speaks of using " the beauties of the earth as steps along which he (the true lover of beauty) mounts upwards for the sake of that other (the divine) beauty, going from one to two, and from two to all fair forms, and from fair forms to fair practices, and from fair practices to fair notions, until from fair notions he arrives at the notion of absolute beauty, and at last knows what the essence of beauty is . . . and so, as a result of that communion, he will be enabled to bring forth, not images of beauty, but realities, and bringing forth and nourishing true virtue, to become the friend of God and be immortal, if mortal man may." [1]

Wherever art, in music, poetry, drama, picture, sculpture, or architecture, succeeds in drawing men nearer to these infinite realms, giving them a deeper perception of the mysteries by which we are surrounded, and, especially in the sphere of dramatic art, a deeper perception and appreciation of the mysterious deeps and heights and potentialities of personality, then it is working hand in hand with ethics, and, indeed, with all that makes for more abundant life. But the very fact that it should so work calls for an intellectual and ethical value-judgment upon it.

[1] *Symposium*, pp. 211, 212. Jowett's translation.

CHAPTER II

THE PROBLEM-PLAY IN RELATION TO SOCIAL AND ECONOMIC PROBLEMS

In this chapter I wish to confine myself to the social and economic problems illustrated by the dramas of Ibsen, Tolstoy, Shaw, and Galsworthy.

Ibsen's standpoint is too well known to need detailed explanation. He was an individualist because he felt that the individual's right to the development of his personality was more important than the rights of society or of the State, and especially the State as then organized. Such plays as *The Pillars of Society*, *An Enemy of the People*, *A Doll's House*, and *Ghosts*, are, in the main, the expression of this idea. After all, we have to recognize, and Ibsen helped people to recognize, that in its attitude to new truth and new developments of thought, what he called the " damned compact majority " is nearly always wrong—simply because it prefers what is " safe," it is not trained to think, or it will not take the trouble to think—and the minority of real truth-seekers, which often begins as a minority of one, is nearly always right. Hence, in matters of thought, but not in matters of conduct, the rights of the individual are sacred as against those of the State. And if the State retorts that it must at all costs protect and preserve itself from what it regards as false or destructive ideas and movements which may lead to anarchy and chaos, the only reply is—so much the worse for the State until it learns to accommodate and adapt itself to the reception and application of new truth. Without an understanding of this position it is impossible for the reader or the hearer of Ibsen's plays to comprehend his point of view, or to understand his attack upon the orthodox conception of the State, or the current ideals which are the foundation of the State, and all its subordinate institutions. The rights of thought, and the rights of personality to the expression of thought, are sacred. They are sacred as against the claims of the individualist State, the Socialist or Marxist State, or the Roman Catholic Church. These are but the passing forms of organization which belong to a particular age. They will pass. But humanity stands for ever, and its very life-breath is freedom to develop.

But there is something more in Ibsen, as we shall see later, than his individualistic condemnation of current ideals of morality and respectability and his protest against current conceptions of State rights. His plea for freedom of opportunity for the development of personality is a much fuller and more positive gospel than at first sight appears. It is a plea for " more abundant life," and we shall see that both his dramas and his gospel were, unconsciously to him, a preparation for the later work of Tolstoy, Shaw, Galsworthy, and many others.

Let us turn, for a moment to the dramas of Tolstoy. Tolstoy did not begin to write plays until he was well past middle life, that is, until some time after his

conversion to a somewhat mystical form of liberal
Christianity based on a literal interpretation of the four
Gospels, and particularly the Sermon on the Mount.
Both his novels and his plays bear the impress of this
conversion. He saw clearly that the whole of society
and of so-called Christian civilization, with its worship
of Mammon and Mars, was animated and controlled by
a spirit directly contrary to that of the Sermon on the
Mount. Three of his plays are worth careful reading :
The Power of Darkness, *The Fruits of Culture*, and *The
Light Shines in Darkness*. I have written of *The Power
of Darkness* elsewhere,[1] so I need not repeat myself here.
It is sufficient to say that the drama is a picture of
Russian peasant life in its most sordid aspects—ignorance,
superstition, poverty, drunkenness, lust, homicide. Yet,
through it all, we are made to feel that peculiar
melancholy and sense of fate which seems to overshadow
Russian life, redeemed by that deep spirit of forgiveness
which so often shines from the human heart where
fatalism is mingled with religion. It is something higher
than Calvinism, for Calvinism, with its doctrine of eternal
torment, is cursed by its conception of a revengeful and
unforgiving God. But the spiritual and dramatic effect
of *The Power of Darkness* can hardly be realized unless
one sees or reads the companion drama, *Fruits of
Culture*. This is a picture of Russian society as it
existed in Tolstoy's time, in its wealth, its luxury, its
corruption, its supposed culture, its false ideas of art
and science, its absorption in trivialities, its waste of

[1] See my book, *The Ethical and Religious Value of the Drama*.

life, its cowardly fear of disease and death. *Fruits of Culture* is the apex, of which *The Power of Darkness* is the base, a god of brass with feet of clay. But still more interesting is the unfinished drama, *The Light Shines in Darkness*. The chief characters are Nicholas Ivánovich and his wife Mary Ivánovna, their family, a tutor, a governess, a priest, aristocratic neighbours, servants, and peasants. Nicholas Ivánovich obviously stands for Tolstoy himself, and the drama represents the contradiction between his inner life, his religious beliefs, and his outward practice, and the terrible clash which results when Nicholas Ivánovich tries to make the one conform to the other, both in his own life and in the home and social life around him. It is a contradiction and a clash which besets and troubles all who have a mind to think and observe and a heart to feel. One or two extracts from the play will bring this home to the reader.

Nicholas Ivánovich is a wealthy landowner, owning some 3,000 acres of forest, containing some 450,000 trees. He is asked to take part in the prosecution of a peasant who has cut down ten of these trees. He refuses.

" Is it worth while to tear a man away from his family and put him in prison for that ? In reality I have no right to this forest. Land belongs to everyone ; or rather, it can't belong to anyone. We have never put any labour into this land. . . . And I didn't preserve the forest myself ! However, this is a matter which can't be proved to anyone who does not himself feel ashamed when he strikes at another man. . . . Just as when a man feels no shame at taking toll from others' labour without doing any work himself, you cannot prove to him that he ought to be ashamed ; and the object of all the Political Economy you learnt at the University is merely to justify the false position in which we live. . . . What is important is that in Yefim's (the peasant's) place I should have acted as he did, and I should have been desperate had I been imprisoned. And as I wish to do to others as I wish them to do to me, I cannot condemn him, but do what I can to save him."

Again, his son, Styopa, wants to enter the Horse Guards as a volunteer, and to do so he must have an allowance. The mother, Mary Ivánovna, pleads that this allowance be granted him, to which Nicholas replies :

" To enter military service of one's own free will I consider either a stupid, insensate action, suitable for a savage if the man does not understand the evil of his action, or despicable if he does it from an interested motive."

MARY IVÁNOVNA.—" After all, he must live."

NICHOLAS.—" I can't give what is not mine. The labour of others does not belong to me. To give him money I must first take it from others. I have no right to do that, and I cannot do it ! As long as I manage the estate I must manage it as my conscience dictates, and I cannot give the fruits of the toil of the over-worked peasants to be spent on the debaucheries of Life-Guardsmen."

Nicholas tries to overcome his scruples of conscience with regard to the use of unearned wealth by proposing that they shall hand over their estate to the peasants, retaining some acres for orchards and kitchen gardens, and live on £50 a year. His wife, Mary Ivánovna, strongly objects. She cannot bring up a family of seven children on £50 a year. Moreover, the drudgery of

such a household, without servants, would kill her.
After an impassioned scene—for husband and wife dearly
love each other—Nicholas agrees to hand over the estate
to his wife, so that he may divorce himself from all
responsibility in the management of it. But this brings
no solution of his difficulties. His neighbours taunt him
with living in a household of luxury, under pretence of
having assigned his estate and his affairs to his wife, and
he feels the taunt. His wife gives a ball, only a dance,
in return for similar invitations the children have received.
One must do these things! But Nicholas can endure
it no longer. He determines to leave home and family,
and another impassioned scene occurs between husband
and wife :

NICHOLAS.—" Mary, you do not need me. Let me go !
I have tried to share your life and to bring it into what for
me constitutes the whole of life, but it is impossible. It only
results in torturing myself and you. I not only torment
myself, but spoil the work I try to accomplish. Everybody
has the right to tell me that I am a hypocrite ; that I talk
but do not act ! That I preach the gospel of poverty while
I live in luxury, pretending that I have given up everything
to my wife."

MARY IVÁNOVNA.—" So you are ashamed of what people
say ? Really, can't you rise above that ? "

NICHOLAS.—" It's not that I am ashamed (though I am
ashamed), but that I am spoiling God's work."

MARY IVÁNOVNA.—" You yourself often say that it (God's
will) fulfils itself despite man's opposition ; but that's not
the point. Tell me, what do you want of me ? "

NICHOLAS.—" Haven't I told you ? You don't wish to
see eye to eye—nor to understand me."

MARY IVÁNOVNA.—" It is not that I don't wish to, but that I can't."

NICHOLAS.—" No, you don't wish to, and we drift further and further apart. Only enter into my feelings ; put yourself for a moment in my place, and you will understand. The whole life here is thoroughly depraved. You are vexed with the expression, but I can give no other name to a life built wholly on robbery ; for the money you live on is taken from the land you have stolen from the peasants. Moreover, I see that this life is demoralizing the children : ' Whoso shall cause one of these little ones to stumble '—and I see how they are perishing and becoming depraved before my very eyes. I cannot bear it when grown-up men dressed up in swallow-tail coats serve us as if they were slaves. Every dinner we have is a torture to me."

MARY IVÁNOVNA.—" But all this was so before. Is it not done by everyone—both here and abroad ? "

NICHOLAS.—" But *I* can't do it. . . . It's just this want of understanding that is so terrible. Take for instance to-day ! I spent this morning at Rzhánov's lodging-house, among the outcasts there ; and I saw an infant literally die of hunger ; a boy suffering from alcoholism ; and a consumptive charwoman rinsing clothes outside in the cold. Then I returned home, and a footman, with a white tie, opens the door for me. I see my son—a mere lad—ordering that footman to fetch him some water ; and I see the army of servants who work for us. . . . All this hurts me very much. Here at home I see a Christmas-tree, a ball, and hundreds of roubles being spent while men are dying of hunger. I cannot live so. Have pity on me. I am worried to death."

The situation is complicated by the fact that an aristocratic friend and neighbour, Boris Cheremshánov, the son of Princess Cheremshánov, has been converted to the religious views of Nicholas ; in other words, he has become a Tolstoyan, and refuses to undergo military training or take the military oath. He is arrested and imprisoned. The Princess calls upon Nicholas, and passionately upbraids him with perverting the morals and religion of her son and ruining his life, and she urges Nicholas to use his influence with the authorities to secure Boris's release.

Unfortunately, the drama was left unfinished, but Tolstoy left a few notes of a draft of the last act. In this draft act we see Boris, with other prisoners from a disciplinary battalion, in a prison cell. He is reading and explaining the Gospel to them. His mother, the Princess, bursts in, but in spite of Boris's protests she is turned out by an officer, and Boris is sent to the penitentiary cell to be flogged. The scene changes, and we see a meeting of the Tsar's Cabinet. The members are joking and smoking cigarettes. Petitioners are announced, among them the Princess, who pleads for the release of her son. Her petition is refused, and she leaves in despair. In the final scene we are back at the country house of Nicholas Ivánovich. Nicholas is ill. The strain has been too much for him. A doctor is in attendance, and, to please his wife, Nicholas consents to take the medicines prescribed. The doctor and the members of the family leave the room for a time, and Nicholas, alone, kneels in prayer. As he prays the Princess bursts into the room with a revolver and shoots him. The members of the household rush in, and Nicholas quietly tells them that he has shot himself by accident. In a few moments he dies, rejoicing that he has done what he could to expose the insincerities of the Church and conventional religion, and that he has understood the meaning and the requirements of life.

I do not know whether anyone has finished this play in accordance with Tolstoy's notes for the final act, nor whether the play has ever been staged in Europe. If not, I hope some one will undertake the work.[1] Despite its didacticism, it is, in my opinion, Tolstoy's greatest drama, and it ought to be played in every town in Christendom. It is a picture of what will happen in thousands of homes in the next generation. Many of the creeds are dying, but the Sermon on the Mount, which represents the realities of religion, has got to be applied in our industrial, social, and political life, if civilization is to endure.

It may be objected, with some truth, that Tolstoy is too destructive, and not sufficiently constructive, in his criticism of existing society and civilization. But the *débris* of an effete and a decaying order of society must be cleared away, at any rate in the region of ideas, before we can begin to build on sound and sure foundations. And Tolstoy has dealt many sledge-hammer blows at the existing order. But no such charge—of mere iconoclasm—can be brought against Bernard Shaw. Shaw has been a tower of strength in the work of both

[1] Since writing this, I hear that the play has been staged in Vienna, and that it is likely to be presented in London during the Tolstoy Centenary, in 1928.

C

destruction and construction. For a more detailed estimate of Shaw's later work I must again refer the reader to my former book on *The Ethical and Religious Value of the Drama*. Here I must restrict myself, for the purpose of illustration, to one play of Shaw's, namely, *Major Barbara*. In this play he is both destructive and constructive—destructive in that he shows how utterly ineffective is a cheap and easy philanthropy for remedying the diseases of civilization ; and, on the other hand, how even the Mammon of Unrighteousness may be turned to righteous uses by a fertile and intelligent mind. The story of the play is simple. Barbara Undershaft, a girl graduate of Newnham College, is the daughter of a millionaire, Andrew Undershaft. This millionaire has made his immense fortune out of munitions—instruments of destruction and death. Barbara, on returning home from college, has taken a religious turn, and, as she is a young woman both of sincerity and of real moral courage, she has joined the Salvation Army in order to bring the great message of salvation and the Gospel to drunkards and sinners and the dwellers in the slums. While she is at the Army barracks one day—a building redolent of the squalor and poverty of the neighbour-hood—Commissioner Baines comes in with the information that Sir Horace Bodger, the famous whisky distiller, has promised them a cheque for £5,000 on condition that they raise other subscriptions of like amount. Undershaft, Barbara's father, who happens to be present, disgusted with the sordid poverty and squalor he sees around him—poor demoralized wretches coming to the shelter, and being served with bread and treacle—immediately caps Bodger's offer with a cheque for another £5,000. Five thousand pounds from profits on whisky! And another five thousand pounds from profits on munitions! Ten thousand pounds from two industries which cause more misery, disease, and death than any other two industries in the world. These munificent donations have a curious effect on Barbara. She is now, as she thinks, deeply and sincerely religious, but her spiritual vision is not very deep or clear. She is curious to see whether the Commissioner, Mrs. Baines, will accept these donations. Of course Mrs. Baines will accept them. Indeed, she is almost ready to sing " Praise God from whom all blessings flow," in her joy at receiving them. But the whole thing is revolting to Barbara. Religion, the holiest and most sacred thing in the world, to be bolstered up by the profits of industries which lead directly to misery, organized slaughter, and death! She will have none of it. And as the officers of the Army prepare to strike up their drums and tambourines and trumpets for the " Glory, Hallelujah," Barbara, in an agony of spiritual despair, cries : " My God, why has Thou forsaken me ? " takes off her Army badge and outfit, and there and then renounces a religion which bases its propaganda and its social work on the profits of misery and slaughter.

In a scene like that, full of scalding satire, we all become, as it were, " guilty creatures sitting at a play," for it is not only the Salvation Army that is involved. All the Churches are involved. And Shaw virtually

shouts at us across the footlights, in the language of
Isaiah :

" Wash you, make you clean.   Take away the evil of your
doings from before Mine eyes."

But the interesting part of the drama lies in the
development of Barbara's personality.   The dear girl
does not see that though she would refuse her father's
£5,000 as a gift for charitable and religious work, she
herself has been indebted all her life long to such profits—
brought up on them, sent to college through them, living
in a fine mansion on them.   Only slowly does she gain
deeper spiritual vision, and the play ends with this fine
speech of hers, in which she rises above the conventional
religion of the time into the prophetic spirit and vision
of all the greater prophets of the world :

" I want all human souls to be saved," she says, " not
weak souls in starved bodies, crying with gratitude for a
scrap of bread and treacle, but full-fed, quarrelsome, uppish
creatures, all standing on their little rights and dignities,
and thinking that my father ought to be greatly obliged to
them for making so much money for him—and so he ought.
That is where salvation is really wanted.   My father shall
never throw it in my teeth again that my converts were
bribed with bread.   I have got rid of the bribe of bread.
I have got rid of the bribe of heaven.   Let God's work be
done for its own sake : the work He had to create *us* to do
because it cannot be done except by living men and women.
For the way of life lies through the raising of hell to heaven
and of man to God, through the unveiling of an eternal light
in the Valley of the Shadow."

The reader will see what I mean when I say that

Shaw, unlike Tolstoy, is both destructive and constructive. Even by the aid of the Mammon of
Unrighteousness, in the person of Undershaft, his mind
is vigilant and alert to point the way to better things.
For when Barbara visits her father's munition works,
expecting to see a group of noisome and pestilential
factories surrounded by workmen's and labourers' hovels
and slum buildings, she finds instead clean, spick-and-
span, well-lighted buildings, to which is attached a
garden city with all the amenities of civilization—a
public library, an art gallery, a concert hall, a theatre,
public and private gardens, playgrounds, baths, clubs,
co-operative associations, and all that helps to make life
healthy, decent, and liveable.   So may even the Mammon
of Unrighteousness, when it has vision and intelligence,
point the way of life to superficial piety and a cheap
and sentimental philanthropy.

On the other hand, John Galsworthy, like Tolstoy,
confines himself mainly to the description of a particular
social atmosphere—as in *The Forsyte Saga*—and the
personalities which are largely the outcome of it.   Nearly
all his plays end with a note of interrogation : " Is this
the sort of life and society with which we ought to be
content ?   Or rather, is it not one of which we ought
to be ashamed ? "   I need only refer to two of his plays
to illustrate my point.   In *Strife*, the story of a strike
in a mining village, we see a whole community held up
by the stubbornness and self-will of two men, the
capitalist Manager-Director of the Company concerned
on the one side, and the Strike-leader of the men on

the other.   After months of suffering and semi-starvation, as a result of which the Shadow of Death finds its way into more than one home, the Managing-Director is deserted by his fellow-directors, and the strike-leader by his fellow-Trade Unionists, and the strike is brought to an end on the very terms which had been suggested by the cool-headed Trade Union Secretary in the early days of the dispute.   The audience is left wondering whether there really can be such a stupid and unintelligent society in existence as one which allows a whole community to be held to ransom, and the mineral resources of the earth locked up, by an insignificant minority in that community !   Truly, as both Voltaire and Bernard Shaw say, this earth must surely be the lunatic asylum for all the other planets !

The Skin Game, the best of Galsworthy's plays, was written shortly after the war.   It is an ironic commentary on the spirit of the " bitter-enders " and the " last shilling " tribe, whose handiwork was seen in the Treaty of Versailles.   Not that the war is mentioned in the play. It is a parable rather of the way in which the bitter-end spirit works in time of peace.   And if in time of peace, to what depths will men descend in time of war !   Mr. Galsworthy prefaces his play with the motto : " Who touches pitch shall be defiled."   That is, whoso orders his life and intercourse with others by the spirit of envy, greed, suspicion, or hatred will ultimately descend to lower deeps still—to the weapons of hatred and the ethics of the Pit—wholesale lying, poison gas, the dropping of bombs on civilian populations, food blockades, and things unmentionable. The drama is really the story of a quarrel between two well-to-do families—one, an old county family of gentlefolk, a Mr. and Mrs. Hillcrist, living in their country house in the South of England ; the other, a family of the " new rich," the head of which is a Mr. Hornblower, a self-made, pushing, and enterprising capitalist who has discovered valuable deposits of clay in the neighbourhood.   Hornblower, to the disgust of the Hillcrists, begins spoiling the whole country-side by erecting pottery factories, and establishing a large industrial centre in close proximity to the Hillcrists' lovely country house. The family trouble begins with Mrs. Hillcrist refusing to call upon the Hornblowers. She looks down upon them, calls them vulgar and common, not proper associates for " gentlefolk." Mr. Hornblower returns this with interest, calls it snobbish. The quarrel becomes more and more embittered. Tenants and dependents are involved, and the venom reaches such a pitch that Hornblower and Mrs. Hillcrist virtually threaten to skin each other in their endeavours to get the better of one another, rather than yield to common sense; hence the title of the play—*The Skin Game*. Matters are complicated by the fact that the younger generation, Jill Hillcrist and Ralph Hornblower, are friendly enough, and are inclined to laugh at the folly and the conventions of their elders. But Mrs. Hillcrist is a determined woman. She has heard some unpleasant scandal about the wife of Hornblower's eldest son. Hornblower laughs the tale to scorn and dares her to do her worst. But she probes into it and determines

to expose the woman. This is too much for Mr.
Hillcrist. To rake into a woman's past, to blight her
present happiness, to ruin her home and her future, is
not, as he says, fit work for gentlefolk. It is touching
pitch. But Mrs. Hillcrist goes on with her unsavoury
work. She brings her agents into the house, gets to
know all the details of the scandal, sends for Mr.
Hornblower, and, after a furious quarrel about a part
of the estate which he has bought, faces him with her
agents' evidence. He sees that he is defeated, but the
extent of his defeat and the nature of Mrs. Hillcrist's
" triumph " is hardly realized until shortly afterwards,
when it is found that young Mrs. Hornblower, having
heard that her long-past secret life has been revealed,
and feeling that her home and her future are now ruined,
has flung herself into the pond at the old gravel pit on
the estate, and the play ends with old Mr. Hillcrist,
bowed in shame, saying :

" What is it that gets loose in us when you begin a fight,
and makes you what you think you're not ? What blinding
evil ! Begin as you may, it ends in this—skin game, skin
game ! When we began this fight we had clean hands—are
they clean now ? "

So might all the belligerent nations in Europe have said
after the war, with their poison gas, their high explosives,
their food blockades, and their holocaust of human life.
Obviously, the play seems to say, if our civilization has
not the intelligence to settle its national and racial
disputes by the methods of mind—by reason, common
sense, and decent feeling, rather than by the methods

of retaliation and the skin game—it will go the way of
the civilizations which have preceded it.

Let me, in conclusion, draw attention to one very
striking fact in connection with these dramas and
dramatists. It is very significant that all of them—Ibsen,
Tolstoy, Shaw, and Galsworthy—base their teaching, in
some form or other, on a central truth laid down by
Jesus the carpenter and Paul the tent-maker. Not the
Golden Rule, for modern psychology, as well as Ibsen
and Shaw, has taught us that " the Golden Rule is
that there is no Golden Rule," that every case is a special
case requiring special treatment according to its individual
needs. No, there is something higher than the Golden
Rule, higher than Kant's universal maxim, " So live that
your example may become a rule of life for others,"
useful though these may be as rough and ready
approximations to justice. There is a passage in Shaw's
Quintessence of Ibsenism which goes to the root of the
matter, and which expresses the central truth of ethical
and spiritual life—a passage which has not received the
attention it deserves :

" Ibsen," says Shaw, " here [in *Little Eyolf*] insists for the
first time that ' we are members one of another,' and that
though the strongest man is he who stands alone, the man
who is standing alone for his own sake solely is literally an
idiot. It is indeed a staring fact in history and contemporary
life that nothing is so gregarious as selfishness, and nothing
so solitary as the selflessness that loathes the word Altruism,
because to it there are no ' others ' : it sees and feels in every
man's case the image of its own. ' Inasmuch as ye have
done it unto one of the least of these My brethren, ye have

done it unto Me ' is not Altruism or Otherism. It is an explicit repudiation of the patronizing notion that ' the least of these ' is *another* to whom you are invited to be very nice and kind ; in short, it accepts entire identification of ' Me ' with ' the least of these.' The fashionably sentimental version, which runs, in effect, ' If you subscribe eighteenpence to give this little dear a day in the country, I shall regard it as a loan of one-and-sixpence to myself ' is really more conceitedly remote from the spirit of the famous Christian saying than even the sham political economy that took in Mr. Gradgrind. There is no hope in individualism for egotism. When a man is at last brought face to face with himself by a brave Individualism, he finds himself face to face, not with an individual, but with a species, and knows that to save himself he must save the race. He can have no life except a share in the life of the community ; and if that life is unhappy and squalid, nothing that he can do to paint and paper and upholster and shut off his little corner of it can really rescue him from it."

" Inasmuch as ye have done it unto one of the least of these My brethren, ye have done it unto Me." That is the central truth in these dramas, as it is the central truth in the teaching of Jesus of Nazareth. The " Me " there stands for the highest thing in the universe, whether we call it the Spirit of Truth, Justice, Beauty, Loving-Kindness, or God. And if that is not at once the central truth in ethics, and the highest form of practical religion, I do not know what religion is. It is the identification of the needs and aspirations of the human spirit with Supreme Love and Wisdom—and all that Love and Wisdom requires of us.

CHAPTER III

THE PROBLEM-PLAY IN RELATION TO SEX AND MARRIAGE PROBLEMS

IT is unfortunate that the term " Problem-Play " has been associated almost wholly with sex - problems. Unfortunate, because there are other problems in life quite as important as the sex-problem. The phrase, also, has unpleasant associations. The application of new truth to life, and especially truth lived, is always unpleasant to the worshippers of the God-of-things-as-they-are, and Mrs. Grundy is always ready to turn up her eyes at what she regards as the least sign of sexual indecorum. The critics, also, have helped in this confusion of thought, for they have too often been the echoes of Mrs. Grundy in these matters, and so have given to sex-problems this false importance.

But in a book which sets itself to deal with the problem-play and its influence on our modern life and civilization, this part of the subject cannot be avoided, and indeed ought not to be. From the preceding chapter the reader will have realized my standpoint. We must try " to see life steadily, and see it whole," or such a measure of the whole as will enable us to form approximately sane and right judgments. If we succeed in doing that, we shall not fall into the error of giving the sex-problem a false importance, though, indeed, our estimate of its importance will vary at different periods of life and will depend largely on our animal and spiritual endowments, our temperament, and our heredity. Like the connected problem of personality it is rooted in mystery, that is, in the nature of things, but we complicate it by all sorts of conventions and taboos which make it a favourite subject for the dramatist.

The sex-problem, as it is reflected in the modern drama, is in part the outcome of the movement for the emancipation of woman, and, in part, a natural rebellion against false conceptions of marriage and the unjust obligations which marriage is held to impose. Ibsen has shown, in drama ·after drama, how the institution of marriage may result in spiritual slavery to false ideals and conventions, and in hypocrisies and insincerities which stunt and deaden the soul. It is surprising how large a number of people there are who still regard woman, not as an end in herself, but as a means for the satisfaction of the wants, comforts, desires, and appetites of man. Ibsen, in one of his plays, in a conversation between father and daughter, shows us the father giving a little moral lecture to his daughter on the duties of woman. She is to be the light and comfort of the home, and, above all, she is to set herself to keep her husband clean and pure. The daughter responds in one word :

" Soap ! "

That is like Ibsen—the concentration of passionate feeling and world-shaking ideas in a word or a phrase. That one word, in the connection in which it is given, and in the crushing nature of the retort, sums up, to a large extent, the cause of the feminist rebellion of the nineteenth century. The best, the most characterful women, determined that they would no longer be regarded as a means, and certainly not as moral cleansers, to minister to the physical and moral welfare of man ; they must be regarded as ends in themselves, standing side by side with man, with the same rights, the same privileges, the same responsibilities, the same spiritual urge towards the complete development of personality. Shaw, dealing with this point in his *Quintessence of Ibsenism*, says : " Unless woman repudiates her womanliness, her duty to her husband, to her children, to society, to the law, and to everyone but herself, she cannot emancipate herself. But her duty to herself is no duty at all, since a debt is cancelled when the debtor and creditor are the same person." Shaw is referring here to the conventional pre-Ibsenite conception of woman as a means, and of woman's duty as a vicarious moral cleanser to man. But he does not show his usual perspicacity in the sentence I have quoted. For modern psychology has shown, as Pirandello has shown in his dramas, that the self, as it at any moment exists, owes a debt to the self which *may* exist, the ideal self, the self which is eternally becoming (I am not quite sure that Pirandello, who is exceedingly pessimistic, would accept this interpretation of his philosophy of life). However, the very idea of moral obligation is destroyed if the possibility of a better, developing self is denied. With all his fanfaronade and tilting against ideals, Shaw, as he

admits, is bound to come back to the ideal in the end.
" The Ideal is dead—long live the Ideal ! " The moment
the self rests in the worship of the God-of-things-as-they-
are, it commits spiritual suicide. It must ever press on
to the worship of the God-of-things-as-they-ought-to-be.
The life of Shaw himself is sufficient commentary on
that text.

It is obvious, then, that for Ibsen these problems of
sex and marriage run down into the deeper problem of
personality. But the interplay of social customs and
conventions, false ideals, and man-made laws, with inner
motives and aspirations, with the inward urge towards
liberation and self-redemption on the part of woman
herself, produces a thousand dramatic and tragic situations of which much of the modern problem-drama is
a reflection. I doubt whether anyone has adequately
voiced the deep spiritual indignation of some of the
best women of the latter half of the nineteenth century,
and of our own time, against the insulting assumption
inherent in the conventional view, and the domestic and
social evils to which those assumptions have led—
indignation against the double standard of morality,
against the idea underlying what is called " the marriage
market " (see the chapter entitled " Clare's Diary "
in George Meredith's *The Ordeal of Richard Feverel*),
against the supposed inherent inferiority of woman,
and especially against the social laws and customs which
place her in a position of economic dependence. Brieux
illustrates this latter problem admirably in his drama,
Woman on her Own, and he is not sparing of the weak-

nesses of woman herself. But there is a great work still to be done in this direction, for there are few causes of matrimonial strife so frequent and so embittering as this of the economic dependence of the wife on the husband. It is possible that the Family Endowment scheme may bring about a better state of things, but all the Family Endowment schemes that I have seen seem to me to avoid the crucial difficulty, and offer only a partial solution of the problem. That is, they lump the mother and the children together, and give the impression that the endowment will meet their needs, leaving the man's income to be dealt with by and for himself. That is, the woman is still dependent, limited to household and economic needs ; the man, with his wage or income, is free. That is not their intention, but it is the impression these schemes leave. In the early years of married life there is often no difficulty. Husband and wife pull together, and the welfare of the growing children keeps them united in sympathies, aim, and endeavour. But as the years pass, and new and diverse interests come into their lives, the woman is often made to feel her dependence upon the good will or otherwise of the man. Perhaps there is no way out of the difficulty save by an ante-nuptial contract which would provide for a periodical division of any surplus of income over household expenditure. But in the millions of cases in which there is no surplus to divide, only mutual kindliness and good will can solve the problem.

But to come back to the more tragic aspects of the problem—for this question of economic dependence *has* its tragic aspects, little realized or known, which the drama has not sufficiently dealt with. No one whose experience has been confined to the average working-class or middle-class suburban home can realize the terrible nature of the evils to which the economic dependence of woman gives rise in other fields of labour and in other parts of the world. The Rev. C. F. Andrews, fellow-worker with Gandhi in India, who has given special study to this matter, writes :

" It has been my duty, in recent years, to make a very careful investigation into the new industrial life of India at the different centres. I have also been called upon to investigate conditions of labour, under indenture, among those who were sent abroad from India to Fiji, Ceylon, Malaya, South Africa, and other places. The facts and figures presented by these investigations have been so startling, as a revelation of festering moral evil, that for a long time I hardly dared to credit them or to give them full publicity. . . . The actual ' Government of India Regulation ' for indentured labour was almost incredible in its callous laxity. It agreed that forty women should be sent out with every hundred men. In earlier years the percentage was thirty-three, or three men with every one woman. These men and women were suddenly swept away from their village homes under these new labour conditions. Very many thousands were thus transported. The result, as I saw it with my own eyes in Fiji, was awful in its moral disaster. The women were compelled to give themselves to prostitution. I will give the picture in the words of Miss Garnham, who was sent by the Australian United Women's Associations, to find out whether my own report was true or false. She writes as follows :
" ' I had evidence from various sources during my stay

in Fiji, that life among the Indian labourers in the " coolie
lines " is unspeakably corrupt. Indians speak of the " lines "
at the mill centres as " prostitution houses " ; and many
men have told me how glad they were to be away from the
" lines," and settle in places where their wives could be
protected. It was quite impossible, they said, for a woman
to preserve her chastity in the " lines." The utter abandon-
ment of morals is unfortunately not confined to the adult
Indians. I have heard little children speak of things which
showed an appalling knowledge of vice of the worst kind.
. . . One may well pause to consider what sort of childhood
is possible where the motherhood is so utterly depraved. . . .

   " ' Moral interests were evidently sacrificed to money
in this labour importation from India ; and the fact that
the prosperity of a colony depends largely on the moral and
social welfare of the people seems to have been disregarded.' " [1]

The results are everywhere the same, and the indentured
labourers take back their habits with them to their homes
and villages in India. And the white man does not escape
the contamination. In certain sparsely settled parts of
Africa, says Mr. Andrews, " there was scarcely one among
the unmarried men, coming as they did from refined European
homes, who did not give way to the temptation of keeping
an African concubine in his house, whom he could never
possibly marry. It was the ' custom of the country.' "

But how can the Drama help in such matters ? It
can help by portraying the tragedies to which the evils
of economic dependence and economic exploitation give
rise ; by tearing the mask of hypocrisy from our civilization
and conventional religion. Mr. John Galsworthy, in his
drama, *The Forest*, has lifted one little corner of the veil
which hides the blood-guiltiness of European civilization,

   [1] *Christ and Labour*, p. 144.

D

and similar work has been done in other dramas by Shaw, Tolstoy, Hauptmann, Brieux, and others.

Let us turn, however, to a more detailed consideration of the problem of sex as it is illustrated by the modern drama. Putting on one side those dramas which introduce the problem of sex simply for sensational and melodramatic purposes, let us consider one or two of the more serious sex-problem plays. These may be divided, roughly, into two or three types : those which are obviously a criticism of present-day conventions and laws ; those which base themselves on the eternal mystery of sex, and, seeing no way out, appeal to our sympathy and our charity when tragic situations and collisions arise ; and those dramas which, rightly or wrongly, try to point the way to better things.

There is a passage in Mr. St. John Ervine's drama, *Jane Clegg*, which illustrates very well what I mean by the first type. Jane has married, in good faith, Henry Clegg, who has had illicit connections with other women both before and after marriage. Jane finds this out, and the question arises—Shall she leave her husband ? The following dialogue occurs between her and Henry's mother, old Mrs. Clegg, who lives with them :

Mrs. Clegg.—" It isn't right to leave your 'usband Till death do you part, that's wot the Bible says."
Jane.—" Why shouldn't I leave him if he isn't loyal ? "
Mrs. Clegg.—" Oh, my dear, 'ow can you ask such a question ? Wotever would people say ? "
Jane.—" But why shouldn't I leave him ? "
Mrs. Clegg.—" Because it isn't right, that's why."
Jane.—" But why isn't it right ? "

Mrs. Clegg.—" You are a one for askin' questions !
Nice thing it would be, I'm sure, if women started leavin'
their 'usbands like that. . . . Doesn't the Bible say you
should take 'im for better or worse ? "

Jane.—" The Prayer Book."

Mrs. Clegg.—" Well, it's the same thing."

Jane.—" I don't care what it says. It isn't right to ask a
woman to take a man for worse. Or a man to take a woman."

Mrs. Clegg.—" But you promised. You knew wot you
was doin' of."

Jane.—" No, I didn't. Do you think I knew that Henry
did that sort of thing, or that I would have married him if
I had ? He married me under false pretences, that's what
he did. He knew that woman before he married me. If he
told a lie about his samples, he'd be put in jail, but no one
thinks anything of his lying to me."

Mrs. Clegg.—" Well, men is men, and there's an end of
it. You just 'ave to put up with them. "

Jane.—" I don't believe in putting up with things unless
you can't help yourself."

That is well put, and it is a perfectly just and damaging
criticism of those conventions which look upon a contract
as sacred even when it has been made under deceitful
and lying conditions which are intended to hoodwink
one of the parties to the bargain. There can be no spiritual
health in a relationship from which love, truth, fidelity,
and honour have departed, and which was founded
originally upon a deceitful contract.

Hindle Wakes, by Stanley Houghton, goes more deeply
into the problem, and is both a criticism and an interrogation. It is well known, but I may recall to the reader
the chief characters and incidents.

Alan Jeffcote, the son of Nathaniel Jeffcote, the millionaire manufacturer of Hindle Vale, has got himself into trouble with Fanny Hawthorne, a weaver in his father's mill. Alan is engaged to Beatrice Farrar, the daughter of a neighbouring wealthy cotton manufacturer, Sir Timothy Farrar. As soon as Nathaniel Jeffcote hears of his son's trouble, he insists, with puritanical sternness, that Alan shall break off his engagement with Beatrice and marry Fanny, the mill-girl, to whom, as the father says, he is " as good as married " already. In this dour proposal he has to face the opposition of his wife, of Beatrice's father, Sir Timothy, an old friend, of Alan his son, and of Fanny herself. The opposition of each is deep-rooted and strong, but springs from varying motives. The double standard of morality comes out clearly. Mrs. Jeffcote, while blaming Alan, sturdily defends his right to marry Beatrice on purely conventional grounds. In these matters, she virtually says, women have to shut their eyes because " men are different from women." The girl " who goes away for a week-end with a man," she says, " cannot be fit to marry our son. It is evident that she is a girl with absolutely no principle "—forgetting, apparently, that " our son " has been as guilty as the girl. Old Tim Farrar objects simply on grounds which usually prompt the roué and the man of the world. Alan objects to marry Fanny because he really loves Beatrice, though he admits that he has been a beast, tempted by the prospect of a week-end's amusement. Beatrice, although she loves Alan, objects to marry him now on religious grounds, and tries to persuade him to marry Fanny, because, after what has happened, he owes it to her to make reparation. That is, she takes Alan's father's point of view for somewhat different reasons. Fanny objects—even with the dazzling prospect of being the wife of a millionaire mill-owner's son being dangled before her eyes—not from any motive of self-sacrifice, but because, being a girl of common sense and stubborn will, she realizes that such a life will not be a happy one, either for herself or for Alan, and because, also, she is not going to sell herself for any amount of money.

In all this tangle of conflicting motives and sex instincts, the only people who command our respect are old Jeffcote, Beatrice, and Fanny. The double standard adopted by Mrs. Jeffcote and old Timothy Farrar is seen to be what it really is—sheer conventionalism on the one hand, and sheer animalism and lust on the other. But we are made to feel also that the rigid standards of Nathaniel Jeffcote and Beatrice would have led to irreparable disaster had they succeeded in persuading Fanny to marry Alan. They are both Puritans in their respective ways, but they are Puritans in a wrong and narrow sense. There is a higher Puritanism than that—the Puritanism which regards the sex instinct as having its rightful place in the world, but that that place is—as we shall see—a subordinate place ; and even when the instinct goes astray, that it must not be allowed to enslave us either to conventions which sometimes issue in lifelong misery, or to habits and customs which drag down the personality and make the ways of the flesh supreme.

There are a good many Fanny Hawthornes in the world, without Fanny's common sense, just as there are a good many Timothy Farrars. Perhaps there are not many women who could have resisted Fanny's temptation to grasp the " eligible " offer which was perforce made to her, for convention, family pressure, and mercenary motives take the most subtle and insidious forms. Ibsen fiercely and ruthlessly exposed such influences, took the mask from their faces, and showed them for what they really were. In *The Lady from the Sea* this subtle huckstering which still goes on in the marriage market is brought out very clearly in the following dialogue :

ELLIDA.—" Now, just listen, Wangel. What is the use of our lying to ourselves—and to each other ? "

WANGEL.—" Lying, do you say ? Is that what we are doing ? "

ELLIDA.—" Yes, that is what we are doing. Or, at any rate, we are hiding the truth. For the truth, the pure, clean truth, is just this, that you came out there—and bought me."

WANGEL.—" Bought ! Do you say ' bought ' ? "

ELLIDA.—" Oh ! I wasn't an atom better than you were. I agreed to it. I went and sold myself to you."

WANGEL.—" Ellida ! Have you really the heart to call it so ? "

ELLIDA.—" But what else can I call it ? You couldn't endure the void in your house. You were looking about for a new wife."

WANGEL.—" And a new mother for my children, Ellida."

ELLIDA.—" Well, perhaps, incidentally, though you hadn't the least idea whether I was fit for the position. You'd only seen me and talked to me once or twice. And you took a fancy to me, and so——"

WANGEL.—" Yes ! call it whatever you please."

ELLIDA.—" And I, on my side—there was I, all helpless and resourceless, and utterly alone. It was so natural for me to fall in—when you came and offered to look after me for all my life."

There are thousands of marriages made under such conditions and with similar motives, and so long as such conditions and motives are allowed to operate they are bound to issue in tragedy.

But let us take a play which, whatever its merits or demerits as drama, does undoubtedly face the whole problem of sex and marriage squarely and openly, namely, Mr. Miles Malleson's drama, *The Fanatics*. Parts of the play seemed to me somewhat turgid, and though the problem is bravely faced, I am not quite sure that the author knows exactly where he stands or what he wants. The play has drawn large houses in London, but as thousands of people have neither seen nor read it, a brief *résumé* of it may be useful here before I proceed to examine its arguments, for it is, above all else, a discussion play.

The scene of the play is a rather sumptuous middle-class house in one of the suburbs of London. Mr. and Mrs. Freeman are discovered just finishing dinner. Mr. Freeman is in a temper because his son John is not attending to business and has coolly walked out of the office that very morning before lunch, and has not done a stroke of work since. When John comes in there is a scene. The trouble is that John has been through the war. He has had his eyes opened, and his conception and estimate of spiritual values are very different from those of his Victorian father and mother. He is a pacifist, and drags in his pacifism, sometimes unnecessarily, to justify his unconventional views about sex and marriage. He makes a convert of his sister Gwen, who loyally stands by him. But he is in trouble also about sex. He has been engaged for some time to Frances Sewell, a friend of the family. But the engagement hangs fire. John has been on active service in France, and has had affairs of the heart with other girls. Even now, while engaged to Frances, he is in love with a musical comedy chorus-girl whom he invites to his rooms in the top flat of the house. There, John's father, Mr. Freeman, discovers them together. The father is furious, and as soon as Frances learns the true state of affairs she breaks off the engagement. In the midst of the scene in which Frances faces John with his unfaithfulness, two of John's friends call, Colin Mackenzie, a successful dramatist, and Margaret Heal, his secretary. Margaret, also, has had " affairs of the heart," and she says that both girls and men often bring their troubles to her. Here, then, these five young people, who represent the younger generation, meet together in John's attic to discuss sex and marriage problems, and as this discussion is the very heart of the play, I must dwell a little upon it.

Margaret has had several lovers, and stands boldly for free love although, as she says, it leads to much bitterness and unfaithfulness. She recounts several of her " experiences," and then :

" Freedom," she says, " is a devastating thing . . . a

few hours I shall never forget, and a year of hell afterwards, and I've never really made up my mind whether I'm glad or sorry."

But she stands, apparently sincerely and wholeheartedly, for free love. Colin, the dramatist, objects to this. " As one gets older and loses one's illusions," he says, " and realizes half one's life has gone, one is apt to get lonely. A lost atom in an infinity of blackness. In that blackness is despair. Only one thing can dispel it—Love. Real love. None of your free sort, John ! . . . Real love isn't free. . . . You can just as easily wreck people's happiness by persuading them to go experimenting all over the place, as by denying them the right to do it."

John retorts that Colin is middle-aged, past his prime, and cannot judge for young people. He is pressed by Colin and the others to state his case, and he does so as follows :

" Well—to start with . . . the obvious things . . . . Hundreds of thousands of girls on the streets ; and an incredible amount of sex disease. One in every five infected ! A million or so girls more than men doomed to a life without love. Some millions of separated people living without love and not allowed to marry again. Thousands of marriages where only distaste and hate remain. Ugliness, and cruelty, and intolerance about the whole subject, that makes the sum of unnecessary suffering almost incredible. Does all that sound like a success ? After all, we're responsible to the next generation for the sort of world they'll find. Have we any right to say : ' Oh, that's all right ; we can't do better than that. We needn't bother.' Look at all the girls in the world : one lot selling themselves to any man who can pay them ; the rest brought up in a sort of prison of asceticism, as candidates for the privilege of becoming a married man's housekeeper."

COLIN.—" Oh, come, John ! Nowadays there are a great many ' betwixt and betweeners,' as it were ! "

JOHN.—" The whole thing's breaking up. . . . The Church is losing its influence. . . . It regards sex as sin. It's holy when the Church permits it in matrimony, and then it's got to remain holy, for ever and ever Amen. . . . The Church built the system, and as a binding force it's no longer effective. Here's your society—in a certain mould ; but the power that did the moulding, that held it together, has gone. It's vaguely keeping its shape, at present—but it's crumbling. It must crumble, and it'll have to be remodelled. That was going on anyhow. Then the war came. Everything shaken to its foundations. Personal beliefs, institutions—everything. The world's fluid. . . . The Church says : ' Society must be purified. Men and women must be taught not to sin.' But what they mean by purifying society is simply forcing it back under the old rules ; what they mean by Sin is any infringement of those rules. What we say is : it's the very narrowness of their rules that has made the mess, it's the reverse side of their mistakenness . . . ' They make of their bodies a rampart for the protection of respectable families,' that's what Balzac says of prostitutes. ' Sacrifices on the altar of monogamy,' Schopenhauer. Prostitution means disease. You *can't* do away with these things by the old rules. The old rules are the *cause* of them. Practice proves it : the countries with easier divorce laws don't have more promiscuity ; less."

COLIN.—" If you had the re-arranging of the world to-morrow, what would you *do* ? "

JOHN.—" There's got to be a religious spirit ; that's essential. I mean the spirit that makes you strive to do the best with your life. . . . I should go all out for a much larger tolerance ; I should allow certain special relationships, *within* the present system, to be open and decent and honourable. . . . Not a trial ' affair.' A trial marriage. We should then definitely find out whether we were suited for life . . ."

COLIN.—" But if ordinary people get into the habit of fluttering from experience to experience they damned easily lose the stability or the capacity for happiness. And undisturbed love between two people is the highest happiness."

GWEN.—" But supposing you don't find it, or make a mistake the first time ? "

COLIN.—" I'm not denying the right of the ordinary person to experiment, but it ought to be for the definite object of discovering a true lover, and making a lasting marriage."

JOHN.—" And if you help people to find their real mates, and when they've made a mistake, help them out of it quietly and decently, you'll have many more happy marriages and much less beastliness."

In the last act we see John's teachings bearing fruit. Rosie, the maid, has a great admiration for the young master, and evidently thinks that no harm can come from putting his teachings into practice. One day Gwen and John find her in tears. She is overcome with shame, and confesses—a baby is coming, and the father is a married man. She talks of suicide. Gwen and John are full of sympathy for the girl and will help her all they can—but they cannot take away her remorse and sense of shame.

Gwen, who stands sturdily by her brother in his spirit of revolt, wants more light on this side of the problem. What is to become of the children in these " trial marriages " ? John's answer is that there needn't be any. " There oughtn't to be any," he says, " until they've set out to be permanent. . . . Nearly everybody, in our class, limit their families." Then he goes on to contrast Rosie's case with what is called " holy matrimony."

JOHN.—" An epileptic woman in a slum can have twelve children by a confirmed drunkard. Which is worse ? That ; or this baby of Rosie's ? But as long as it's in ' holy matrimony,' people can have dozens of children with no earthly chance of looking after them—and your moralists make no objection ; but they'll torture young Rosie till she thinks of suicide. . . . The whole question of children—I'm sure it's a matter of *clear thinking*. It's so damned important we should think clearly. . . . Love between two people is a personal relationship."

GWEN.—" Yes."

JOHN.—" I can't see that anybody has a right to interfere."

GWEN.—" No."

JOHN.—" But as soon as you have a child, it's more than personal ; it's a social relationship."

GWEN.—" Yes."

JOHN.—" And the Law oughtn't to be concerned with the personal side of it at all ; but with the social—with the obligations to the children. . . . What Rosie knows, she knows from cinemas, and giggling talks with other girls and occasional young men. . . . About the real possibilities of life, and its real dangers, she knew nothing ; and along comes this man ; and over she goes ! . . . If she'd belonged to us, she'd have known what she was doing. . . . Now that it *has* happened, half her trouble is her *fear* ; the disgrace of it. If instead of cursing her, and blaming her, and pushing her away, people would help her, it wouldn't be so very terrible."

The situation becomes still further complicated when it is found that Gwen and Colin, the dramatist, have fallen in love with each other, but that Gwen refuses to go through the form of marriage until she is more sure that a permanent union will turn out satisfactory. That is, she wants a " trial marriage," and is quite willing to " go away " with Colin on that understanding. Colin is nonplussed, and hesitates to compromise the girl. The father, when he learns the state of affairs, is furious. " Wanton, cruel, insane folly " . . . " insane wickedness that I never thought I should find in a child of mine " . . . " trampling on everything we hold sacred." John stands faithfully by Gwen, and Colin ultimately gives way; and the play ends in a confused sort of way—the stage version somewhat differently from the published version—with Mr. Freeman in a fury and Mrs. Freeman so wrapped up in her innocent Victorian ideals that she trips about the stage in delight, finding it impossible to believe that anything other than a real marriage is intended.

The conflict of ideals is obvious, and it is equally obvious that it is based on sincerity of spirit, even though it be an inexperienced sincerity on all sides. The weakness of John's position may be illustrated by a sentence from Ibsen's *The Master Builder*. When Solness says to Hilda Wangel :

" *Could* you come to love a man like that ? "

Hilda replies :

" Good heavens ! You know very well one cannot choose whom one's going to love."

SOLNESS.—" Oh, no, I suppose it's the troll within one that's responsible for that."

That is true, but it is only half a truth. " I do not like thee, Dr. Fell, the reason why I cannot tell," etc.

But though we cannot always choose whom we can love, we *can* choose whether we will give way to sex-passion or not when the impulse prompts us. There are two mistaken assumptions underlying John's long argument. First, he confuses sex-passion with Love. But Love is something more than sex-passion, though it may include sex-passion. Second, he assumes that sex-passion, being a natural instinct like hunger, should, when necessary, be satisfied like hunger. But just as there are moral conditions imposed upon the satisfaction of the instinct and desire for food, so there are moral conditions imposed on the satisfaction of the instinct and the desire for sex-passion. Both instincts are natural and legitimate. But as we should never think of satisfying either hunger or thirst—particularly in time of famine—without consideration for others, or at the expense of others, so we cannot legitimately satisfy the sex-instinct without observing the conditions which make for a higher order of relationships than those of the hen-coop, and a higher type of spiritual nature than mere sex-passion produces. It is here that Bernard Shaw, great as is our debt to him, sometimes confuses his readers and unwittingly leads them astray. He will persist in belittling the word Love because it is so often used in a sentimental and romantic sense, and he writes sometimes as though sex-passion alone were to be described as Love. But great words are the possession of mankind, and their meaning should not be limited to the narrow conceptions and usage of any particular school. The love of the mother for her child ; of the artist and the poet for his ideal; of the philosopher for Truth; of the martyr for his cause, are something far greater and higher than sex-love, great as this may be. The warning word here is surely that of Plato—Restraint. The winged steeds of the soul, Passion and Aspiration, must be guided by the charioteer Wisdom. But alas! Wisdom is learned too often only by sad experience.

And this brings me to our final play in this chapter, namely, Ibsen's *When We Dead Awaken*, a play which was the fruit of the great dramatist's ripest wisdom and long years of experience. The play is purely allegorical—an epilogue, as Ibsen himself called it, to his own life and work, containing his last commentary on Art and Love. In this allegory he deals imaginatively with two of the greatest problems of life, and gives his judgment upon them. First, he affirms that Art is not an end in itself, but that it must be subordinated to Life. Not " Art for Art's sake " must be our motto, but Art for Life's sake. Second, he teaches that sex-passion must in the course of experience be sublimated, not by celibacy, but by a finer passion produced by a union of Love with Wisdom. But this finer passion, inwrought with Wisdom, comes only with age, when passion, in the lower sense, is dead! But let us get to the play, so that I may bring home to the reader the final message, on this matter, of one of our greatest modern dramatists.

Arnold Rubek, the chief character in the play, is a sculptor. For years he has been filled with the idea of a statue which will be his supreme achievement in life.

It is a vision of " The Resurrection Day." It is to be
embodied in the form of a woman awakening from the
sleep of death—an awakening which is to typify the
purest and most ideal womanhood, a woman " filled with
a sacred joy at finding herself unchanged in the higher,
freer, happier regions, after the long dreamless sleep
of death." He finds his inspiration in a beautiful woman
named Irene, who becomes his model.

" Thus did I fashion her—I fashioned her in your image,
Irene."

And having so fashioned his vision, he treats Irene,
his model and inspiration, as a mere means to his art,
and virtually dismisses her with the words : " I thank
you for a priceless *episode*." The word stings. What
has been a mere episode to the artist—an episode which
will bring him riches and fame—has been as the drawing
of her heart's blood to the soul of the woman. She drops
out of his life for a time, and is driven to seek a living by
posing at variety theatres, by vice, by sensual living,
winning rich men by her beauty and luring them to their
doom. Meanwhile, Rubek marries a sensuous, pleasure-
loving girl, Maia, a being symbolical both of the beauty
and the passion of the life of Spring-time—a union of
Art and Pleasure. But such passion, unguided and
uncontrolled by wisdom, cannot last, and, ere many
years elapse, Rubek and Maia become intolerably bored
with each other. Rubek loses his inspiration. His art
becomes degraded. He himself, with success, becomes
cynical and materialistic, and his degenerate nature

begins to show itself in his work. He is no longer satisfied with his statue, which has hitherto represented something spiritual and divine, and he changes it into a group which has in it something evil and malign. He introduces himself into the group, then portrait busts behind the faces of which " there is something equivocal, something cryptic—a secret something that the people themselves cannot see "—something of the animal which is in most men—" respectable, pompous horsefaces, and self-opinionated donkey-muzzles, and lop-eared, low-browed dog skulls and fatted swine snouts, and sometimes dull, brutal bull-fronts as well . . . the animals which men have bedevilled in their own image, and which have bedevilled men in return."

This is the pre-drama spiritual development of Rubek, necessary to the understanding of the play. The scene of the play, for the most part, is a mountain health-resort, whither Rubek and Maia have gone in their travels, to escape from their boredom with each other. Maia becomes entangled with Ulfheim, a hunter, a man more gross and sensual than herself, but who relieves her of her tedium with Rubek. Then Irene, broken in mind and body, appears with her nurse, and in a scene which becomes tense and tragic, and almost inexpressible with deep feeling, we see the retribution which has fallen on them both. In bitter words Irene describes the causes which have led to it. The statue she regards as her spiritual child—*their* child.

IRENE.—" I fell down at your feet and served you, Arnold ! But you—you—you—— ! "

E

RUBEK.—" I never did you wrong ! Never, Irene ! "

IRENE.—" Yes, you did ! You did wrong to my innermost, unborn nature—— "

RUBEK (*starting back*).—" I—— ! "

IRENE.—" Yes, you ! I exposed myself wholly and unreservedly to your gaze —— "

RUBEK.—" I was an artist, Irene."

IRENE.—" That is just it. That is just it. . . . The work of art first, then the human being."

RUBEK.—" You must judge me as you will ; but at that time I was utterly dominated by my great task—and exultantly happy in it."

IRENE.—" And you achieved your great task, Arnold."

RUBEK.—" Thanks and praise be to you, I achieved my great task. I wanted to embody the pure woman as I saw her awakening on the Resurrection Day . . . filled with a sacred joy at finding herself unchanged—she, the woman of earth—in a higher, happier, freer region—after the long, dreamless sleep of death. I fashioned her in your image, Irene."

IRENE.—" And then you were done with me. . . . But you have forgotten the most precious gift."

RUBEK.—" The most precious—— ? What gift was that ? "

IRENE.—" I gave you my young, living soul. And that gift left me empty within—soul-less. (*Looking at him with a fixed stare.*) It was that I died of, Arnold. . . . When I had served you with my soul and with my body—when the statue stood there finished—our child, as you call it—then I laid at your feet the most precious sacrifice of all—by effacing myself for all time . . ."

RUBEK.—" Was it jealousy that moved you then ? "

IRENE (*coldly*).—" I think it was rather hatred."

RUBEK.—" Hatred ! Hatred for me ? "

IRENE.—" Yes, for you—for the artist who had so lightly and carelessly taken a warm-blooded body, a young human life, and worn the soul out of it—because you needed it for a work of art."

Irene here illustrates what Ella, in another of Ibsen's dramas, says to Borkman : " The Bible speaks of a mysterious sin for which there is no forgiveness. I have never understood what it could be ; but now I understand. The great, the unpardonable sin, is to murder the love-life in a human soul."

This dialogue with Irene brings home to Rubek what has long been smouldering within him and quickening and torturing his conscience. He feels that he has suffered degradation both within himself and in his art ; that he has been guilty of the ruin of another soul. Only by rising above this " death in sin " can the dead awaken. The play ends in symbol and mystery. Both couples, Maia and Ulfheim, and Irene and Rubek, make an expedition up the mountain, the former in search of pleasure and sunlight and freedom ; the latter to find the promised land of the Spirit—shall we say the spirit of peace, or the spirit of struggle and possible achievement towards a fuller development of personality ? But a storm descends upon the mountain. Maia and Ulfheim, coming down to seek shelter and safety from the coming dangers of mist and snow, meet Irene and Rubek ascending, and try to persuade them to return. But the latter are now above all earthly fears—they have found the secret of the awakening from the dead, and are ready to meet physical death itself if need be. They prefer to face the danger of death in order that they may reach the mountain-top which symbolizes the promised land of the Spirit, where, through the mists, life may be transfigured by sunshine. But the storm continues, and soon a sound like thunder is heard high up on the mountain-side above them. And as the avalanche comes with rushing speed upon them and buries them beneath its enormous mass, the play ends with the cry of the Sister of Mercy—Irene's nurse, who, at some distance, has followed them up the mountain—the cry, " Pax vobiscum."

One might say that while, with Dante, love, at its highest, ends in ecstasy, an ecstasy too great for mortal mind to bear, with Ibsen love ends in mystery. Shall I say spiritual mystery ? For the final words of the play, " Pax vobiscum," seem to point to an ideal of spiritual peace and repose in some other sphere of being.

Here, then, are four plays, each of which has a distinct message on the problem we are considering. Let me try, briefly, to summarize the message of each, so that we may see their relation to each other and to the problem of sex itself.

In *Jane Clegg* we have the natural and obvious ethical principle enforced that a contract, to be binding, should be based on truth and sincerity, not on falsehood, and the more sacred the contract the deeper the responsibility for openness and truth. In *Hindle Wakes* the suggestion is made that sex-passion, especially in its aberrations, should not necessarily determine the lifelong contract of marriage. Passion cannot always decide things wisely. Everyone with any experience of life knows that young people, as they pass into manhood or womanhood, sometimes " fall in love," as the saying goes, many times over. It is Nature driving the sexes together for her own purposes. Young lovers are apt to call it " the hand

of God," and to say, in their new-found joy, that their
marriage has been " arranged in heaven." But how
many of these early ill-assorted unions end in the divorce
court ! Not that we need necessarily set our faces against
early marriages, provided that there is a deeper love
than mere sex-passion—a love which we may call understanding love, uniting two personalities of like tastes and
sympathies. In *Hindle Wakes* the situation is saved
and a misalliance prevented by the sturdy common sense
of Fanny. In *The Fanatics* the whole problem is laid
bare. The evils of a false and conventional system which
allows for no rectification of the misguidings of passion
are exposed, but there is little or no constructive suggestion. The argument of the play, as expressed by the
chief character, is vitiated by the assumption—not
stated, and sometimes qualified—that because the sex-
instinct is a natural instinct it is therefore right to gratify
it without consideration or observance of the conditions
which society imposes for the general good. Such an
assumption would lead to the indiscriminate multipli-
cation of the unfit, the feeble-minded, and the mentally
degenerate, who most easily give way to sex-passion,
and who are frequently the most prolific of their kind.
What the conditions which society may impose *should
be* is, of course, a matter for discussion. But here the
play fails us. In *When we Dead Awaken*, Ibsen gives us,
not perhaps in his best dramatic form, the gathered
wisdom of his declining years, and that wisdom takes
the form of the sublimation of the sex-instinct and the
ending of a finer spiritual love in mystery. Here, also,

we gain little help. For we cannot put old heads on young shoulders, or expect wisdom, where wisdom is not, to take the guidance of passion. It is all very well for men like Ibsen and Tolstoy, in their declining years, when they have passed through the storm and stress of life and passion—it is all very well for them to preach the sublimation of the lower instincts. Truly, that is necessary. But the trouble is that at certain ages and periods Nature laughs at sublimation, and concerns herself only with the reproduction of life by instincts which, in youth, sometimes seem almost uncontrollable.

Is mystery, then, our last word ? I fear it is. Mystery—and Restraint. And the deeper we pursue the subject the deeper does the mystery become. Experts in the physiology of sex now tell us that, while the human organism may be male or female, the glandular secretions sometimes determine the sex-instincts, propensities, and affections in an abnormal way, and in a reverse direction to the physical or physiological indications. That is, a female may have masculine instincts and propensities, and a male may have feminine instincts and propensities, thus producing a type which, in some cases may be asexual, and in others homosexual or homogenetic. Readers of Edward Carpenter's strange and interesting book, *The Intermediate Sex*, will know what I mean. The information Carpenter gives, based on expert authority, throws light on several dark and mysterious phenomena in this connection. It may help to explain that, to us, strange and extraordinary custom, *paiderastia*, which was so widely prevalent in the life

and civilization of the ancient Greeks. Carpenter
contends that this intermediate sex may shadow forth a
new type of human being—a higher and more heavenly
type. Indeed, they are called Uranians, or Ouranians—
from the Greek word *ouranos* (heaven)—and certainly
the fact that some of our greatest geniuses have been
men of this type, and that others have been more or less
variations of the type, lends colour to Mr. Carpenter's
suggestion. My own experience of such people is too
limited to be of much value. But from what I know, I
may say that some of these people are so extraordinarily
gentle and lovable, so magnetic in spirit and personality,
and, even in their aberrations, so supreme in their
particular genius and way or art of life, that they
deepen our reverence for human nature and our
sense of the mystery which surrounds this problem
of sex.

As one rises from a study of the chief sex-problem
plays and the best sex-problem literature of our time,
one feels that every writer, every dramatist, is limited
or conditioned, perhaps I should say pre-determined, by
his temperament, his instincts, his spiritual constitution
—the intertwining influences and conflicting " ghosts "
of dead ancestors—in all his judgments. This is, of
course, inevitable. In this matter we cannot " see life
steadily and see it whole." We see only a fragment, and
our perception of that fragment is coloured by the psychic
conditions which are part of our being, or warped by
the experiences through which we have passed. Hence,
the endless variety of masculine judgments on woman—

a saint, or a temptress ; a ministering angel, or a worldly
schemer ; a romantic personification of the Ideal, or
a Becky Sharp—and all the varieties that lie between these
extremes. Think of a few of the great writers and dramatists who have given their judgments to the world on what
is called the " woman question " and the problem of
sex. Goethe, Schopenhauer, Shelley, Tolstoy, Nietzsche,
Wagner, Ibsen, Strindberg, Shaw, Havelock Ellis—
how their judgments differ according to the personal
idiosyncrasies and experiences of each one of them !
We see at once how dangerous the generalizations
even of great men may be, and though we welcome
their dramas and studies as reflections upon and interpretations of a great problem and a great mystery, we
feel that there is something behind which eludes and
escapes them all. But the careful student will find
in two or three of them—in Havelock Ellis, Ibsen,
Bernard Shaw, and Edward Carpenter—indications of
a point of view and an attitude of mind towards which
the best men and women are moving, and which will
enable him to test the worth of the meretricious and
sensational sex-problem plays which too often find their
way on to the stage. An attitude of mind which, while
allowing for the human allurements, temptations, appetites, and passions of the Venusberg, yet sees that that
is but a stage in human development, and that for each
one of us there is a deeper and a richer life, to the realization of which the sex-passion must be subordinated if
we would live our life at its best. The aim of Love, at
its highest, is to spiritualize life. But sex-passion, though

it may aid in this, may also, if it is uncontrolled or misdirected, debase and brutalize life. There is something wider and deeper, something which cannot be restricted to the narrow channels of personal, family, or even racial affections and affinities ; something to which we can hardly give a name without raising questions of definition—but something to which we have to win through—loving-kindness, friendliness, the " fellowship which is Heaven, and the lack of which is Hell," comradeship, loyal service and devotion to a great cause which we may call Truth, Beauty, Righteousness, Humanity, as we list. These, not passionate, romantic love, in the ecstatic transports of which it would be impossible for human beings to live permanently and retain their sanity—these are the permanent, the enduring things, by which humanity really lives. And when these higher things have taken possession of one's heart and mind, and the lower passion-driven love becomes ordered and transfigured by them, then loving-kindness, deep *understanding* love, a union of sympathy, grace, and wisdom, become the master-powers of the soul. The final question will always arise : Are we to be the slaves of Nature, blind and passion-driven, or are we to be rational, self-conscious, responsible co-workers with her ?—intelligent souls co-operating with her in her purposes towards an end which, wherever intelligence is at work, has something of prevision in it, by which to guide our efforts and our struggles.

The reader will see from this the direction in which the better sex-problem dramas of our time are leading us—the liberation of the human mind from false ideas, immoral customs, and degrading insincerities and hypocrisies. But just as the bioscope, the music-hall, and the novel sometimes pander to the sensational and the suggestive, to the lustful and animal side of human nature, so the sex-problem drama may do the same, lending itself, in the name of Realism, to the description of unpleasant and pornographic episodes. We must trust, however, to the healthy common sense in human nature and to the education of the public taste, and not be too squeamish in our censorships. The common law against indecency should be enough.

The pessimistic view of the sex-problem may be seen in the dramas of Strindberg, particularly in his dramas *The Father* and *There are Crimes and Crimes*— exceedingly clever, but dominated by a perverse and morbidly fatalistic spirit ; and also in Hauptmann's *The Reconciliation* and *Lonely Life*, plays which end in a kind of mysticism. Out of this clash of opinion, of feeling, and of types of character, good will come. What the ultimate result will be on the institution of marriage it is impossible to say. But we have to bear in mind that in this matter salvation must come from within, not from without, and, as Bernard Shaw truly says, speaking of Ibsen, we must continue to protest, with him, " against the ordinary assumption that there are certain moral institutions which justify all means used to maintain them, and insist that the supreme end shall be the inspired, eternal, ever-growing one, not the external, unchanging, artificial one ; not the letter, but the spirit ;

not the contract, but the object of the contract ; not the abstract law, but the living will."

And in all these things much must be left to the privacy of the individual judgment. We know too little of each other's inner life, too little of each other's " defects of will and taints of blood " to set ourselves up as moral censors in these matters. Cruelty, hypocrisy, lust, suborning, the " marriage market, " the economic dependence which leads to the enslavement of the will —these we can always fight against. But as for the rest, the incident recorded in the eighth chapter of John has its lesson for all of us, men and women alike. And in all our striving and our reforming let us remember that institutions and customs are to be judged by their effects upon personality. Do they promote chastity, self-control, the subordination of appetite to the wiser mind and will, of flesh to spirit ?   And do they promote the fullest development of personality ?   If not, the Time-Spirit has already touched them with its wand.

In all this the drama can help us, has helped us.   Consider the great women characters of Shakespeare—their superb sanity, their healthy, spiritual vitality, their intellectual strength.   Or consider, in a different field, the women of George Meredith's novels, prophetic of women who were to come, and perhaps of greater immediate spiritual influence than some of Shakespeare's creations, because they were nearer to the conditions and circumstances of our own life and time.   About some of Ibsen's and Shaw's women there may be something harsh and repellent, because they were created in a time of struggle and conflict, and conflict brings out the harsher and harder side of human nature. But women like Agnes Brand, Major Barbara, Lavinia, Candida, and many others bring a breath as of mountain air into our mental and spiritual life. In these ways the drama, even the sex-problem drama, helps us—by making us ashamed of our insincerities and hypocrisies, our mean restrictions and jealousies, our ignoble and narrow conceptions of love, our low ideals of manly and womanly comradeship. Every time we are brought back to the one great aim—the transfiguration of love and the development of personality by experience, tragic or otherwise, as the case may be.

But when all is said, the last word, in sex as in life, is Mystery. And, with our little minds, what else could it be ? As Mr. J. D. Beresford, in that remarkable but too little known novel, *The Hampdenshire Wonder*, says :

" Oh, pity the child for whom there could be no mystery. Is not mystery the first and greatest joy of life ? Beyond the gate there is unexplored mystery for us in our childhood. When that is explored, there are new and wonderful possibilities beyond the hills, then beyond the sea, beyond the known world, in the everyday chances and movements of the unknown life in which we are circumstanced. . . . Don't you see that ignorance is the means of our intellectual pleasure ? It is the solving of the problem that brings enjoyment—the solved problem has no further interest. When everything is known, the stimulus of action ceases ; all that remains is quiescence, nothingness. Perfect knowledge implies the peace of death, implies the state of being one—our pleasures are derived from action, from difference, from heterogeneity. Surely we should all perish through sheer inanity, or die desperately by suicide if no mystery remained in the world."

CHAPTER IV

THE PROBLEM-PLAY IN RELATION TO ETHICAL AND RELIGIOUS PROBLEMS

I

THE EUMENIDES OF ÆSCHYLUS.
THE PURIFICATION OF THE IDEA OF GOD.

IT is now common knowledge that the best drama is intimately connected with religion, and especially with the ethical side of religion ; that the ancient Greek drama sprang out of religious dances, choric chants and odes, and religious ritual ; and that ethical and religious ideas have had a great influence, in every age, on the drama and on the development of drama. For a fuller and more detailed treatment of this subject I must refer the reader to my books, *The Ethical and Religious Value of the Drama*, and *Drama, Music-drama, and Religion*.

Much will depend, of course, on the meaning we attach to the word "religion." It is a grave mistake to give a narrow meaning to great words, and the word " religion " has suffered much in this way. As Bernard Shaw truly and trenchantly says :

" Pray, what are the mysteries of religion ? Are they faith, hope, love, heroism, life, creation ; or are they pews and pulpits, prayer-books and Sunday bonnets, copes and stoles and dalmatics ? Even that large section of the population whose religion is the merest idolatry of material symbols will not deny that the former are the realities of religion. Then I ask the gentlemen who think that the pews and prayer-books are too sacred to be represented on the stage, why it is that they have never protested against the fact that all our dramas deal with faith, hope, love, and the rest of the essentials ? . . . The objection made to Mr. Henry Jones's play (*Michael and his Lost Angel*) is really an objection to Michael's treatment of religion as co-extensive with life : that is, as genuinely catholic. To the man who regards religion as only a watertight Sunday compartment of social observance, such a view is not only inconvenient but positively terrifying. I am sorry for him ; but I can assure ·him that the British drama is annexing steadily the territory on which he feels so comfortable. And whoever tries to obstruct that advance will be inevitably ground into the mud."

This intimate connection between the drama and religion has again been brought into public notice by the recently published translation of *The Eumenides* of Æschylus by Professor Gilbert Murray. Professor Murray draws special attention to this in his preface to the play. Indeed, the great Greek dramatists, Æschylus, Sophocles, and Euripides, like the Greek philosophers, seemed to be trying to bring into the minds of their hearers and readers a juster, a more humane conception of the Supreme Spirit, than that which had hitherto existed. Essentially, on its ethical side, through Art, their work and purpose was similar to that of the Hebrew prophets. If it be true that God makes man in His own spiritual image, it is equally true that man makes his gods in his own image, and in time of persecution and war a ghastly image it is. For when men begin to kill each other either on a large or a small scale, it is usually done with the sanction of their priesthoods and under the supposed commands of their God. And even in time of peace the ethical problems of punishment, retribution, atonement, mercy, forgiveness, and reconciliation are intimately connected with man's conception of the Divine Spirit or the Divine nature, and its requirements. We see this clearly in the development of religion, both in the Old and in the New Testament ; and we may see it clearly also in this drama of Æschylus, *The Eumenides.*

Let me try to bring before the reader the chief circumstances and incidents in the drama, on which the ethical problem turns, and by which, also, the dramatist is trying to insinuate into the minds and hearts of his hearers, by means of great Art, a purer and more merciful conception of the Divine Spirit.

In ancient times the doctrine that sin must bring punishment and that " the doer must suffer " was expressed in the formula " blood for blood," " An eye for an eye, and a tooth for a tooth." But if blood is always to be shed for blood, where is bloodshed to cease ? The same problem besets us in war. Hatred and vengeance can find no way out. Æschylus tries to find a way. The situation on which the drama is based is this.

Clytemnestra, in guilty complicity with Ægisthus, murders her husband Agamemnon. Orestes, her son,

constitutes himself the avenger, and slays his mother—
blood for blood. But who shall bring vengeance and
punishment to Orestes ?—for matricide is the most fearful
of crimes ! The Erinyes, the pursuing Furies, acting
as the " wrathful hounds " of the dead, the spirits which
encompass and ensure the doom of the sin-stricken and
the earth-bound—these are the supposed messengers of
Zeus, the Most High, whose duty it is to exact blood
for blood. Orestes seeks to escape the wrath of the
Furies, and the play opens at the Temple of Apollo at
Delphi, with Orestes seeking asylum at the altar in the
inner shrine of the Temple. The Furies lie sleeping
around him, charmed to slumber by Apollo, the son and
messenger of Zeus. Apollo appears and bids Orestes
fly to the Temple of Athena in Athens, where just
judgment shall be given him. As Orestes departs the
Ghost of Clytemnestra appears, and, with taunts and
cries of vengeance, urges the Furies to their work.
Apollo drives them from the sacred " Temple of Mercy,"
and they fill the air with their rage and their curses,
determined to " hunt him to the grave," for blood must
have blood—and the scene closes with the words of
Apollo, a new note in ancient theology :

> " 'Tis mine, then, to bring succour, and to save
> My suppliant. Earth and Heaven are both afraid
> For God's wrath, if one helpless is betrayed."

The scene then changes to the Temple of Athena in
Athens, where Orestes bows, a suppliant, before the
statue of Athena Parthenos. Years have passed, and
Orestes is worn with travel and suffering. As he prays

to the goddess for help the Furies come to seize their
prey, chanting their song of doom :

> " Up, let us tread the dance, and wind—
>   The hour is come !—our shuddering spell.
>   Show how this Band apportions well
> Their fated burdens to mankind.

> " Behold, we are righteous utterly.
>   The man whose hand is clean, no wrath
>   From us shall follow ; down his path
> He goeth from all evil free.

> But whoso slays and hides withal
>   His red hand, swift before his eyes
>   True witness for the dead we rise :
> We are with him to the end of all."

    ✱   ✱   ✱   ✱   ✱

> " Thus hath Fate, through weal and woe,
> For our Portion as we go
>   Spun the thread :
> Whenso mortal man in sin,
> 'Brueth hand against his kin,
> Mine till death He wandereth,
> And freedom never more shall win,
>   Not when dead.

> " But our sacrifice to bind,
>   Lo, the music that we wind,
>   How it dazeth and amazeth
>   And the will it maketh blind,
>   As it moves without a lyre
>   To the throb of my desire ;
>   'Tis a chain about the brain,
>   'Tis a wasting of mankind.

    ✱   ✱   ✱   ✱   ✱

" For so it abideth : subtle are we to plan,
    Sure to fulfil, and forget not any Sin ;
    And Venerable they call us, but none can win
    Our pardon for child of man."

Thus the Furies stand for the old Law of vengeance,
" As a man soweth, that shall he also reap " ; they stand
for custom, for tradition—blood for blood, " An eye for
an eye, and a tooth for a tooth."

But as they finish their song and dance Athena appears,
Athena, the daughter and messenger of Zeus. Orestes
has appealed to her in her Temple, and he shall have
judgment and justice. " Strange man," she says, turning
to Orestes, " and what in turn hast thou to advance ? "

Orestes states his case. His father, Agamemnon, the
" marshal of a thousand ships," returning home from the
wars after sore suffering, is received as with honour by
his wife Clytemnestra, " black of heart," who snared and
entangled him in the nets and curtains of the bath to
which she led him. Exiled many years, but spurred on
by Loxias, the prophet of Zeus, Orestes returned and
slew his guilty mother :

    " Take me thou, and judge if ill
I wrought or righteously. I will be still
And praise thy judgment, whatsoe'er betide."

To which Athena replies :

    " This is a mystery graver to decide
    Than mortal dreameth."

Yes, the mystery of duly-apportioned guilt, allowing
for extenuating circumstances, hereditary predispositions,

motives, conscience, exaction of due penalty, penance, suffering, forgiveness. Yet, even the Furies she cannot slight—in the half-blind minds of the people they, too, are as the messengers of the Gods to execute due vengeance.

ATHENA

" Doubtful thus it lies . . .
Myself not judging, I will judges find
In mine own City, who will make no blind
Oath-challenge to pursuer and pursued,
But follow this new rule, by me indued
As law for ever. Proofs and witnesses
Call ye on either side, and set to these
Your oaths. Such oath helps Justice in her need.
  I will go choose the noblest of the breed
Of Athens, and here bring them to decide
This bloody judgment even as truth is tried,
And then, their oath accomplished, to depart,
Right done, and no transgression in their heart."

The Furies are amazed. What " new rule " is this ? What are whys and wherefores, motives and intentions to them ? The deed is done, the doer must suffer— blood for blood. Custom, tradition, law demand it. If sin and crime go unpunished the very bonds of society will be loosened. Again they join in Chorus :

" This day there is a new Order born.
  If this long coil of judging and of strife
  Shall uplift the mother-murderer to life,
Shall the World not mark it, and in scorn
  Go forth to do evil with a smile ? "

But the word of Athena, the goddess, has gone forth, and in the next scene we are in the Council Hall of the

Areopagus at Athens, and before us are Athena, Apollo,
the Judges, the Furies, Orestes, a Herald, and a crowd
of Citizens. The argument between prosecution and
defence, the Leader of the Furies and Orestes, is
difficult to summarize, it is so concentrated and closely
interwoven. Orestes admits his deed. The Leader
presses for punishment ; if punishment does not follow
sin as a bond, where shall they look for Justice ? Apollo
steps in with the reminder :

> " Bonds can be loosened ; there is cure therefor,
> And many and many a plan in God's great mind
> To free the prisoners whom he erst did bind."

In the end the Judges cast their pebbles, for or against
the prisoner. They are found to be equal, and Athena,
as the messenger of Zeus, gives the casting vote in favour
of Orestes.

The Furies again give vent to their rage in chorus :

> " Woe on you, woe, ye younger gods !
> Ye have trampled the great Laws of old
> Beneath your chariots ! Ye have broke the rods
> Of justice, yea, and torn them from my hold !
> Mine office gone, unhappy and angered sore,
> I rage alone. What have I any more
> To do ? Or be ? Shall not mine injury turn
> And crush this people ? Shall not poison rain
> Upon them, even the poison of this pain
> Wherewith my heart doth burn ? "

But Athena, the Goddess of Wisdom, turns to them
with her powers of gentleness and persuasion :

> " Ah, take thought ! Nor on our heads
> Rain the strange dew a spirit's anger sheds,
> Seed-ravening blight and mildews merciless,
> Till all the land lie waste in fruitlessness.
> Spare us, and, lo, I promise : here shall be
>   A home your own, a caverned mystery,
> Where alway ye shall sit, enthroned in pride
> And shining, by my people glorified."

Again and again do the Furies rage, and again and again does Athena meet them with arts and arguments of persuasion, pointing out that the spirit and the deeds of gentleness, reverence, and understanding love are mightier and fuller of blessing than the spirit of hate and vengeance. These gifts and blessings shall be theirs when they have rid themselves of the poisonous spirit of hate, and they shall be transformed from the Furies into the Eumenides—the Kindly Ones who bring spiritual health, blessing, and salvation. At last the Furies are appeased. On them, too, the wise and beautiful city has its claim, and at last they sing :

> " Let manhood's glory by no doom
>   Of death untimely be defiled ;
> Let life to maidens in their bloom
>   Bring each a lover and a child.
> O whatsoever Gods have power,
> And Fates eternal, grant this dower !
> *   *   *   *   *
> " Let her who hungereth still for wrong,
>   Faction, in Athens ne'er again
> Lift on the air her ravening song ;
>   Let not the dust of Pallas' Plain
> Drink the dark blood of any son
> By fury of revenge foredone.

" Rage not to smite the smiter, lest
    By rage the City's heart be torn :
    Bless him that blesseth : in each breast
So shall a single love be born."

To which Athena responds :

" Wise are they and have found the way
    Of peace. And in each awful face
    I see for you, my People, grace :
If ye are gentle, even as they,

" And do them worship, this shall be
    Your work : to guide through ill, through good,
    Both land and town in that pure mood
Of truth that shuns iniquity."

And to the Furies she says :

" Fare ye well also. I must go
    Before you, guiding, to make bright
    Your secret chambers with the light,
The holy light, they dared not know.

" Come, and when deep beneath the veil
    Of earth ye pass, 'mid offering high,
    Hold down the evil that shall die,
Send up the good that shall prevail."

The Furies have been transformed into the Eumenides,
the Kindly Ones, the bringers of blessing, and the drama
ends with a chorus of joy from a procession of citizens
that

" The Law that is Fate, and the Father
    the All-Comprehending,
Are here met together as one."

This bare summary does scant justice both to the argument of Æschylus and to our indebtedness to Professor Gilbert Murray. But it will enable the reader to realize how the dramatist is striving to bring into the mind of his hearers a juster, a higher conception of God. Law is blind. And custom and tradition based on Law are blind. Law generalizes. It cannot discriminate. It cannot pierce with compassion to the heart. It cannot therefore allow for individual weaknesses, for heredity, for extenuating circumstances and conditions. As Professor Murray himself points out in his Introduction to the play, quoting Plato's *Statesman* : " The best of all is not that a law should rule, but a man, if the man be wise and of royal nature. . . . A law can never comprehend exactly what is noblest and most just for all cases, and consequently cannot enjoin what is best. The infinite varieties of men and circumstances, and the fact that nothing human ever for a moment stands still, make it impossible for any art to lay down a simple rule to hold universally and for all time. . . . But that is what we see the Law aiming at, like some stubborn and ignorant man who will allow nothing to be done against his orders, and no further question to be asked." That is, Æschylus, and, after him, Sophocles and Euripides, were striving to do in the realm of dramatic art what Socrates, Plato, and Aristotle tried to do in the realm of ethics and philosophy.

But we shall see this development of ethical and religious feeling and thought more clearly if we turn for a moment to the Bible, and watch the same development

and struggle going on in Hebrew and Christian thought.
There, too, we meet with the same cry, " The doer must
suffer," " blood for blood," " an eye for an eye, and
a tooth for a tooth." To obtain purity a sacrifice is
required, individual, and sometimes national. In extreme
cases, among both Greeks and Hebrews and other races,
a human sacrifice is offered, as in the case of Iphigenia
and Jephthah's daughter. Then animal sacrifices and
the first-fruits of the harvest take the place of human
sacrifices, until, as we reach the higher prophetic teaching,
the law of sacrifice is assigned second place to ethics or
is actually contemned. " Bring no more vain oblations ;
incense is an abomination unto Me." " The sacrifices
of God are a broken spirit." But custom and tradition
die hard, and even in Paul—adapting himself, perhaps,
to the hereditary and traditional theological prejudices
of his hearers—we find a harking back to the idea that
sin can only be cleansed, and forgiveness won, by a
sacrifice of blood—" the blood of Christ," and his
tortuous reasoning leads him into the dialectical morass
from which comes his frightful declaration, " God hath
mercy on whom He will, and whom He will He
hardeneth."

No, it is to the spiritual genius of Jesus of Nazareth
that we must turn if we would find the purest development of Christian ethics. There, the Law of outward
sacrifices is banished, the Temple, figuratively speaking,
comes down with a crash, and the inner sacrifices of the
heart give a new life to religion and to humanity.
Spiritual insight, mercy, compassion, patience, wisdom,

understanding love, take the place of the hardness and
uniformity of Law. When, in reply to Peter's question,
" How oft shall my brother sin against me, and I forgive
him—until seven times ? " Jesus says : " I say not unto
thee, Until seven times ; but Until seventy times seven,"
he is simply emphasizing, in a figurative and exaggerated
way, the ethical requirement that we must never leave
a single human soul to pursue its own destruction, but
rather that we must bring all our powers of " gentle
persuasion " and love to bear upon it. But Jesus is no
sentimentalist. He lays down two conditions ere forgiveness can be expected and purity attained. First, as
in the parable of the Unjust Steward, that we must be
prepared to forgive others ere we can expect forgiveness ourselves. Second—and much harder and more
important—the moment experience and suffering bring
light into the darker realms of the soul, there must be
a welcoming of the light and a deliberate turning to the
better way. That, surely, is the meaning of the parable
of the Prodigal Son. The moment the Prodigal comes
to himself—his better self—the moment he realizes how
dreary and miserable his life of sensuality and self-
indulgence really is, and turns to the better way, that
moment the work of forgiveness has begun, and there
is no more to be said, but feasting and rejoicing. Every
student of psychology knows that all these words and
feelings represent a long cycle in the development of
personality ; blindness, or want of perception, selfishness
as a result of that blindness, egotism, then the reper-
cussions of experience which bring the suspicion that

excess or lust of any kind is unsatisfying and unhealthy, then the suffering which brings light, then contrition, remorse, penance, a desire for forgiveness, and a deliberate turning to the better way.

Just as Æschylus, Sophocles, and Euripides, by their dramatic art, sought to bring into the human mind a deeper sensitiveness to the ethical requirements of the Supreme Spirit, so the same need exists in our own age. However far the children of men may seem to drift away from the paths of righteousness and decent living, the true father-and-mother heart in the Community—Athena's " Guardian of the City "—will yearn over the lost, yearn to protect them from irredeemable evil, and warn them against the pitfalls into which any one of us may so easily fall. For good or ill we are identified with the life of humanity as a whole, " members one of another." We are bound together by unseen, but irrevocable bonds, and from earliest youth

> " Our acts our angels are, or good or ill,
>   The fatal shadows that walk by us still."

Nay, that couplet does not go far enough, for our deeds, or the ghosts of them, walk not only *by us*, but by our children also, and the spirit which lived and moved in our ancestors lives and moves—but let us hope, transformed and transmuted—in us also.

Let the reader carry this idea one step farther, and he will begin to realize something of the full meaning of the word " forgiveness " and of the problem which beset Æschylus. For if there is such a thing as Spirit in the

Universe, a Spirit of whose Life we are the offspring, and if there is such a thing as righteousness and loving-kindness attaching to that spirit, then the same spiritual links that bind our children to us, also bind our lives to the Parent-Spirit of the Universe. And just as, in thought and affection, we will never let our children go permanently away from us, but will follow them in wonder, in sorrow, or in love wherever they may be, so we may surely conceive that the Parent-Spirit will never let any portion of humanity go permanently away from It [1] into irretrievable ruin. It follows us like " The Hound of Heaven." The spiritual laws are never in a hurry, they can afford to wait. But the *road* to forgiveness is always open. Theologians talk much about the grace of God, and they say that that grace can only be obtained on the terms which are laid down in their creeds. That is not so. The grace of the Spirit is a free gift. It is like the sunshine and the refreshing rain which stream down upon all—upon the evil and the good, the just and the unjust alike—with this difference : that we must turn our hearts towards it ere we can receive its fertilizing power. The ethical law itself is grace. Always that grace may be ours, not as the result of a transaction between an Almighty Despot and an erring slave, but as a spiritual development towards self-identification

---

[1] The reader will probably object to the word " It " in this connection. But I use the impersonal rather than the personal pronoun so as not to confuse thought. The Spirit, or a spiritual interpretation of the universe, is the thing that matters. I think Emerson is right when he says that Spirit must include all that we mean by personality, but must be more than personal, that is, super-personal.

with those higher laws and spiritual powers of the universe which, through much suffering and deep mystery, are drawing mankind towards purer heights of Being than we yet know. We must have faith in that, else life has no meaning.

But still the mystery remains, and will ever remain : the mystery as to how light can be brought to the darkened and unreceptive mind. It may be that in ways and spheres of which we can only speak in figure and parable—the Valley of Humiliation, or the Valley of Suffering and the Shadow of Death—the deeps will be broken up, and the blind or darkened soul will realize its need for light, until, through new developments in the depth and tenderness of its nature, it learns to fear to hinder, or injure, or in any way taint or clog the mighty stream of Being of which it is a part ; until it feels, in its utter self-identification with the Spirit of Life, that if it injures that Spirit even in " one of the least of these " it injures its own very self and life. For the Kingdom of the Spirit is indeed within us, and must continue to be within us as a great yearning ere it can come to its fullest consummation and realization outside us as a great fact.

Civilization is passing through this cycle of experience now. It has fed, like the Prodigal Son, and is still feeding, on husks, or trying to find satisfaction in the accumulation of wealth, in luxuries, in new sensations, and all manner of excess. Even the shock of the war and its aftermath has not awakened it to health and sanity. But there are signs, here and there, that it is dimly groping after the light, that it is striving to find and apply the spirit which Æschylus and the great Greek dramatists, and Socrates, and Plato, and Aristotle, and Jesus of Nazareth strove to introduce into the hearts of the peoples, the religions, and the gods of their day—the spirit of what Æschylus calls " gentle persuasion," and what Jesus of Nazareth calls the Spirit of Truth and understanding Love. For we are slowly learning, even in our schools, that the child-soul must be awakened and developed, not regimented ; in our prisons that the uniformity of punishment and of Law must give way to the investigations of the trained psychiatrist, the probation system, the industrial school, and the Borstal system ; and in our manufacturing industries that the needs and instincts of the human soul come before the requirements of mass-production and the tyranny of the machine. But the old gods are not dethroned in a day, and their worshippers, in their blindness, cling tenaciously and even with religious or scientific fervour, as the case may be, to custom and tradition. The outlook is dark, and the tragedy of Socrates and of Jesus, or even of Babylon, Greece, and Rome, may again be enacted in somewhat different form.

But I think I have said enough to show that the problem which Æschylus and, after him, Sophocles and Euripides set themselves to solve, was a real problem, that it goes to the roots of religion and to the ideas which lie behind the great words—retribution, atonement, salvation, forgiveness, reconciliation ; and that we are strangers to the full meaning and requirements of these words until the spirit of the Eumenides, the Kindly Ones, enters into our hearts. In these matters " every man must be a priest unto his own soul."

II

BERNARD SHAW'S *THE SHEWING-UP OF BLANCO POSNET.*
THE PROBLEM OF " GRACE."

Fundamentally, Bernard Shaw, in most of his dramas, is trying to do what Æschylus and all the great dramatists and prophets did in their day. He is trying to give to men clearer conceptions of what the Supreme Spirit, which he calls the Life-Force, requires of them ere they can attain to " more abundant life." For the mere externals of religion—candles and vestments, ritual and ceremonial—he has scant reverence. He pierces at once to the essentials, and to illustrate these essentials he usually makes his chief characters either heretics or rebels to the conventional beliefs and customs of their day. " Every genuinely religious person," he says, " is a heretic." And undoubtedly Shaw, despite his heresies, or perhaps I should say because of his heresies, conjoined with deep spiritual insight, is a genuinely religious person. That is why orthodox religious people on the one hand, and the rationalists and the agnostics on the other, have never been quite able to understand him, or have been continually irritated by him. The orthodox people do not like his apparent lack of reverence for things which they deem sacred, to which he would retort that they show something worse than lack of reverence for the things which he deems sacred ; and the rationalists and agnostics do not like his use of the words " religion " and " God." And looking back upon human history, and upon the many things that have been done in the name of God, one can partly understand their prejudices. But neither our prejudices, nor the narrowness and bigotry of professedly religious people, should blind us to the true meaning and value of great words. The word religion certainly requires purifying from its unwholesome accretions, but it is too valuable a word to be thrown on the scrap-heap. And though there may be much difference of opinion about the word " God," if Shaw prefers to use the term " Life-Force," as Matthew Arnold preferred to use the phrase, " the Eternal not ourselves which makes for righteousness," or as Herbert Spencer preferred the phrase, " the Infinite and Eternal Energy from which all things proceed " —who shall say them nay ? Jesus of Nazareth defined God as Spirit (" God is Spirit ")—a great definition— and there are many people who prefer the term Spirit, and who find in it deeper meanings than they find in the term " God."

The careful reader of Bernard Shaw cannot but be struck by the frequency with which Shaw, like Ruskin, expresses himself in the language of Jesus, Paul, and sometimes of Bunyan. His mind and spiritual nature are simply saturated with the spirit which gave birth to the New Testament—apart, of course, from its legendary and adventitious accretions. That is because his spirit derives from the same spiritual type, and therefore drinks at the same spiritual source. This may sound like great praise, but it is not intended as praise at all. Shaw's religious spirit is simply an illustration of the spiritual mystery which theologians call "grace," the mystery with which *The Shewing-up of Blanco Posnet* specially deals.

It is impossible to understand Shaw's religious point of view without getting first a clear understanding of the meaning of that passage from *The Quintessence of Ibsenism*, which I quoted on pp. 41-42, and to which I must again ask the reader's attention. In that passage Shaw is really expressing himself in the terms of the parable of the Last Judgment, and he is using almost the very language of Jesus as interpreted by his most mystical apostle, John. In that passage, Shaw, like Jesus, rises above all "otherness," above even the rather fatalistic limitations of the Golden Rule, into the region of one-ness with the Spirit of Life, claiming the opportunities of attaining that one-ness, with all its spiritual treasures and values, *for all*. If the reader will realize what the passage means when applied to economics and politics, he will see that it implies both a social and a religious revolution in thought and life.

On the purely theological side Shaw bases his religion on the theory that the Life-Force is striving, through the law of evolution and development—evolution as interpreted by Samuel Butler rather than by Darwin— striving, through trial and error, to redeem its apparent failures, and to bring to birth ever higher and more perfect types of life. Its failures are the mastodon and the ichthyosaurus—extinct types—the cancer microbe, and the tuberculosis germ. Its successes are a Pythagoras, a Socrates, a Plato, an Aristotle, and a Jesus, and all the subordinate types, in mankind and in flower and forest, which add to the joy and beauty of life, and which bring joy, beauty, and strength—fuller life—into the lives of others.

The Shewing-up of Blanco Posnet is intended to illustrate the way in which the Life-Force, the Spirit, deals with the apparently unredeemable, and the apparently irreclaimable—the type of character whom the revivalist preacher and the Salvation Army love to bring up to the penitent form. The play, strangely enough, was censored in Great Britain for many years, and is probably not so well known as many others of Shaw's plays. I must therefore trespass on the patience of those of my readers who have seen or read the play, so that I may make its story and its central problem clear to those who have not.

The scene of the play is fixed in a rough pioneering settlement in the wild West of America. It opens in a large barn-like room which serves both as a meeting-house and a court-house. A horse has been stolen, and Blanco Posnet, a rough scapegrace of a man, is charged with the theft. The penalty in the settlement for stealing a horse is hanging, or shooting, or both together, for the loss of a horse in those days meant loss of transport, and loss of transport meant lack of food and the necessaries of life. Blanco is brought into court. The

women of the place, whom Shaw has made to match
the men, receive him with ribald cries of " Horse thief,"
" Hang him," " Lynch him "—" the varmint." To all
which, Blanco, who has had some education in his youth,
responds :

> " ' Angels ever bright and fair.' "

BETSY (*one of the women*).—" If you call me an angel, I'll
smack your dirty face for you."

BLANCO.—" ' Take, oh, take me to your care.' "

EMMA.—" There won't be any angels where you're
going to."

Blanco's supercilious attitude and retorts so exasperate
the women that they make a rush at him, tear his clothes
and scratch his face, and have to be pulled back by the
men. When order is restored Blanco again derisively
responds :

> " ' Oh, woman, in our hours of ease,
> Uncertain, coy, and hard to please—'

" Is my face scratched ? "

> " ' When pain and anguish wring the brow,
> A ministering angel thou ! ' "

In this way the Court of Justice is prepared for the trial.
Before the trial begins, however, the religious leader
of the settlement, Elder Daniels, tries to bring Blanco
to a repentant frame of mind by pious exhortations.
But that is hopeless, for Blanco knows Elder Daniels,
the reformed drunkard, better than he knows himself.
As a matter of fact, Elder Daniels is Blanco's own
brother, trading under an assumed name, but Blanco

is too contemptuous of the whole settlement and the life of the place to give him away. The Elder puts Blanco's ribaldry and bravado down to spiritual pride, and says he will end on the gallows tree. But Blanco retorts that God hasn't finished with the Elder yet. Hypocrisy and whining sentimentality will not always have its own way.

"God's a sly one," says Blanco. "He lies low for you. He lets you run loose until you think you're shut of Him, and then, when you least expect it, He's got you. . . . That's how He caught me, and put my neck in the halter. To spite me because I had no use for Him—because I lived my life in my own way and would have no truck with His ' Don't do this,' and ' You mustn't do that,' and ' You'll go to Hell if you do the other.' I gave Him the go-by and did without Him all these years. But He caught me out at last. The laugh is with Him as far as hanging me goes."

ELDER DANIELS.—" Don't dare to put the theft on Him, man. It was the Devil tempted you to steal the horse."

BLANCO.—" Not a bit of it. Neither God nor Devil tempted me to take the horse : I took it on my own. He had a cleverer trick than that ready for me. Gosh, when I think that I might have been safe, and fifty miles away by now, with that horse, and here I am waiting to be hung up and filled with lead ! What came to me ? What made me such a fool ? That's what I want to know. That's the great secret."

It is that secret which the trial is to bring out, and it is a secret for which Blanco will hang ten times over, if that were possible, rather than confess it.

The Sheriff, a beef-faced, thick-necked bulldog sort of man, comes in and takes his place, and the trial begins. The Sheriff asks the prisoner if he has settled his affairs, if he is in a proper state of mind, in other words, if the Elder has had a spiritual talk with him—to which Blanco replies : " Yes, and it's torture. It's against the law for prisoners to be talked to and tortured like that. Let the trial begin."

The trial does begin, and the Sheriff calls for witnesses. But the only witness who professes to have seen Blanco with the horse on the morning of the theft is a Feemy Evans, a woman who has taken the primrose path, and who is of so dubious a character that the Sheriff refuses to accept her evidence as good enough on which to hang a man. No one else has seen Blanco with the horse. When he was arrested there was no horse to be seen near him, and he himself seemed to be " kind of moon-struck," says Strapper Kemp, " because when we took him he was gazing up at a rainbow in the sky !"

It seems as though Blanco would be acquitted, or that they would have to hang him on Feemy Evans's tainted evidence. But just then a commotion is heard at the door of the court. Messengers of the court have found the horse, and they've found the apparent thief. It is a woman. As soon as Blanco sees her he loses all his bravado, and looks terror-stricken.

The woman takes her place as a witness. She wears an expression of intense grief, which silences the court. The Sheriff asks her what she is doing with a horse that doesn't belong to her.

THE WOMAN.—" I took it to save my child's life. I thought it would get me to a doctor in time. My child was choking with croup."

Then they question her as to how she got the horse.

" I got it," she says, " from a man that met me. I thought God sent him to me, and I rode here joyfully thinking so all the time to myself. . . . The man looked a bad man. He cursed me ; and he cursed the child : God forgive him. But something came over him. I was desperate. I put the child in his arms ; and it got its little fingers down his neck and called him Daddy, and tried to kiss him ; for it was not right in its head with the fever. He said it was a little Judas kid, and that it was betraying him with a kiss, and that he'd swing for it. And then he gave me the horse, and went away crying and laughing, and singing dreadful, dirty, wicked words to hymn tunes, like as if he had seven devils in him ? "

THE COURT.—" Was that the man ? " (*pointing to Blanco*).

The woman looks scaredly at Blanco, then at the bull-necked Sheriff, then at the rough devil-may-care jury eager for a hanging—and then says, " No ! "

It is now a choice between the word of a disreputable woman, Feemy Evans, whom nobody trusts, and this stranger, stricken with grief, who has just lost her child, for the child, after all, is dead.

Feemy Evans is put in the witness-box again, this time under oath. But lo ! she, too, turns " softy." After fumbling and vacillating a good deal, she says it wasn't Blanco that she saw. She only said it out of spite because he had insulted her. " May I be struck dead if ever I saw him with the horse."

What is this ? It is the Life-Force, God, " the Eternal not ourselves," the Spirit of Loving-kindness, or what- ever the reader may please to call it, getting at these **rough people's hearts** through a stricken mother with a dying baby. The Sheriff declares Blanco free, and Blanco mounts the table, and points the moral in this wise :

" Dearly beloved brethren," to which the boys respond : " Same to you, Blanco. Lord, have mercy on us, miserable sinners."

BLANCO.—" No ; that's where you're wrong. Don't flatter yourselves that you're miserable sinners. Am I a miserable sinner ? No ; I'm a fraud and a failure. . . . I'm a rottener fraud and failure than the Elder here. And you're all as rotten as me. There's none of us real good and none of us real bad."

ELDER DANIELS.—" There is One above, Blanco."

BLANCO.—" What do you know about Him ? You that always talk as if He never did anything without asking your rotten leave first ? Why did the child die ? Tell me that if you can. He can't have wanted to kill the child. Why did He make me go soft on the child if He was going hard on it Himself ? Why should He go hard on the innocent kid and go soft on a rotten thing like me ? Why did I go soft myself ? Why did the Sheriff go soft ? Why did Feemy go soft ? What's this game that upsets our game ? For seems to me there's two games being played. Our game is a rotten game that makes me feel I'm dirt and that you're all as rotten dirt as me. T'other game may be a silly game, but it ain't rotten. When the Sheriff played it he stopped being rotten. When Feemy played it the paint nearly dropped off her face. When I played it I cursed myself for a fool ; but I lost the rotten feel all the same."

ELDER DANIELS.—" It was the Lord speaking to your soul, Blanco.

BLANCO.—" Oh, yes. You know all about the Lord, don't you ? You're in the Lord's confidence. He wouldn't for the world do anything to shock you, would He, Boozy dear ? Yah, what about the croup ? It was early days when He made the croup, I guess. It was the best He could think of then ; but when it turned out wrong on His hands He made you and me to fight the croup for Him. You bet He didn't make us for nothing ; and He wouldn't have made us at all if He could have done His work without us. By gum, that must be what we're for ! He'd never have made us to be rotten drunken blackguards like me, and good-for-nothing rips like Feemy. He made me because He had a job for me. He let me run loose till the job was ready ; and then I had to go along and do it, hanging or no hanging. And I tell you, it didn't feel rotten : it felt bully, just bully. Anyhow, I got the rotten feel off me for a minute of my life ; and I'll go through fire to get it off me again."

And the play ends with Blanco standing drinks all round, and offering to shake hands with Feemy Evans.

The reader will now see what I mean when I say that it is quite impossible for the average theatre-goer to understand, to the full, this little play unless he knows something of Shaw's ethical and religious standpoint, and unless he realizes the meaning of that passage (already quoted [1]) in *The Quintessence of Ibsenism*, that all Life is one in Spirit, and that any mean or selfish act we do to any humblest fraction of it is done to the Spirit of Life, that is, to God Himself, and, through Him, to ourselves and the community in which we live. Take the war, which might well be termed the crucifixion of the Spirit, and which has been called an exemplification of the parable of Blanco Posnet on a large scale. There, too, to adopt for a moment Blanco's style of

[1] *Ante*, pp. 41-42.

speech, there was a great game, and a rotten game
played. The great game was that played by the idealistic
youth of Europe, the young men of every nation, who,
misled or coerced by their rulers, went forth to the cry :
" Our country is in danger ; " " Never again ; " " It
is a war to end war ; " and died by the million, sometimes mad with pain, or with the thought and the scene
of their old home in their dying eyes and memory, and
wondering, like little Peterkin, what would come of it
all. And the " rotten game " was that played by the
stay-at-homes who made profit out of the bloodshed,
and who calmly and placidly, or with tortured hearts,
accepted the terrible sacrifices of their young as something unavoidable or divinely ordained—the game played
by the statesmen, the diplomats, the politicians, and the
preachers—the Strapper Kemps and the Elder Danielses
—who painted the so-called glories of war in romantic
colours and talked about it as being the Will of One
above, and dressed it up in religious robes, and honours,
and ribands, and stars, and crosses, as though it were
a lovely and holy thing instead of a foul and beastly
thing. War will never be seen to be the evil thing it
is until men realize this one-ness of Life expressed in
the great sentence : " Inasmuch as ye did these things
unto one of these My brethren, even these least, ye did
them unto Me."

Or consider the theological side of the play. The
Life-Force, God, sends the croup, the cancer microbe,
the tuberculosis germ, but, in the course of evolution,
by experiment, trial, and error, He sends something to

fight croup and cancer and tuberculosis. Note that sentence of Blanco's : " He wouldn't have made us at all if He could have done His work without us "—what is that but a popular variant of George Eliot's well-known saying : " Even God Himself could not make a Stradivarius without Antonio Stradivari ? " and of the Apostle Paul's theology on its best side : " We are God's fellow-workers. Know ye not that ye are a temple of God, and that the spirit of God dwelleth in you ? " But here, also, there is a great game and a foul game to be played. The great game is to fight croup, and cancer, and tuberculosis cleanly and courageously, by clean, healthy, and rational ways of life and proper sanitation ; the foul game is to fight it by binding down animals with steel wires, or otherwise making them entirely helpless and defenceless ; burning, scalding, mutilating, or otherwise torturing dogs, horses, cats, rabbits, rats, mice, squirrels until they become stupefied, imbecile, or mad ; injecting their filthy serums and so-called anti-toxins into human beings, and then excusing and covering our meanness, our cowardice, and our cruelty by saying that it is for the benefit of humanity—as though any decent-minded human creature would wish to benefit by such means ! Yes, the game of life is bound up with the way in which we answer all these questions—that is, bound up with science, art, ethics, and religion.

And there is the problem of Blanco himself. Why should the Life-Force take the trouble to bring such an apparently disreputable specimen of humanity back to playing the *great* game rather than the " rotten " game

of life ? Is it not to show mankind, through the spirit
of the prophet, the poet, or the dramatist, how the Way,
the Truth, and the Life works ? Not merely by
revivalist meetings, and threats of eternal damnation,
and sickly sentimentalist talk which too often sounds
like cant ; nor by imprisonment within stone walls with
their treadmills, and cat-o'-nine-tails, and opium-picking,
and solitary confinement ; but by a psychology which
studies the temperament, the heredity, the mental and
spiritual twists and peculiarities of the criminal, and
then sets itself to train him to see what is really decent
and healthy and sane in life, and what is ugly and hateful
—just as all that was best in Blanco Posnet was brought
out by a woman with a dying baby, and so shamed him
out of his " rotten " way of playing the game of life.
It is the Spirit of Loving-kindness which Æschylus
and Bernard Shaw are trying to bring home to their
hearers and readers in these plays, and which Shakespeare
himself emphasizes when, in his final message, he tells
us that

" The rarer action is
In virtue than in vengeance."

Surely it is obvious that these things go to the very
roots of Theology and Ethics. And yet people say that
Bernard Shaw is blasphemous and irreligious ! So it
was said of Isaiah, Jeremiah, Socrates, and Jesus of
Nazareth, and the tragedy which ensued was the natural
consequence of intolerance, and the bitterness and
hatred which too often accompanies the intellectual
blindness which cannot perceive or appreciate new

truth. Even in our own day men like Tolstoy, Gandhi, and Bernard Shaw would receive short shrift from the worshippers of Mammon and the God-of-things-as-they-are. Well does Shaw say, with scathing irony, that there is no hope for a nation which revises its Parish Councils and Parliaments once every three or five years, but will not revise its creeds once in fifteen hundred years.

Bernard Shaw's religion is based on all that is best in the great world-religions, East and West, but interpreted and expounded with his peculiar genius.

First, that the Life-Force, God, the Spirit of Life, is One.

Second, that mankind, being born of the Spirit of Life, are *children of the Spirit*, and therefore are fellow-workers with him, " members one of another."

Third, that we can only " live righteously," and play the great game towards that Spirit of Life, by identifying ourselves with it. Not by otherism, or altruism, or philanthropy, or any other of the fine self-glorifying names with which we clothe our spiritual pride and think we are religious when we are only sentimental and conventionally pious and self-seeking, and trying to escape the obligations of real religion by donations to charitable institutions which will take off our hands the unpleasant and disagreeable work of cleansing and healing the sores and wounds of the body politic, which our own selfishness or thoughtless negligence may have caused. In other words : " Inasmuch as ye did these things— these mean, and low, and base things, or these great and high things—unto one of these My brethren, even these least, ye did them unto Me "—the Spirit which is Life.

That is the teaching of the dramas of Æschylus, Ibsen, Tolstoy, Galsworthy, and Shaw.

III

SOMERSET MAUGHAM'S *THE UNKNOWN*. THE PROBLEM OF AGNOSTICISM.

In a foreword to this play Mr. Maugham tells his readers that he has tried to put into dramatic form some of the thoughts and feelings which have agitated the minds of many people during and since the Great War. One of the characters in the play is a clergyman, and Mr. Maugham says that the speeches he has put into the mouth of this clergyman are taken largely from the writings of prominent clergymen and theologians in the Church of England, so he thinks he cannot be charged with misrepresenting their point of view. Mr. Maugham's play brings home to us the devastating effects which the war has had on the religious beliefs of large numbers of people. Its criticism of existing beliefs, or rather of beliefs which prevailed very widely up to the time of the war, is mainly destructive, whereas Shaw's criticism is both destructive and constructive. But destruction of false ideas and beliefs is necessary before true ideas can take their place, and this play should help many who are seeking firm and clear ground for the foundations of a new faith to see how necessary it is that they should first rid their minds of the false idols and beliefs of the past.

The scene of the play is fixed in the country-house of a well-to-do middle-class English family in Kent. Colonel Wharton, the father, is a retired soldier, and his son John, Major Wharton, is home from the front on leave. He is engaged to Sylvia Bullough, a near neighbour, and the marriage is to take place almost immediately, before Major Wharton returns to the front. But a few days after John's return home the vicar of the parish calls, and the talk gradually drifts on to the subject of the war and its connection with religion. The vicar, the Rev. Norman Poole, becomes rather enthusiastic about war, praises it as " a great school of character, where, amid the clash of arms, the great Christian virtues —courage, self-sacrifice, charity, self-reliance—shine forth with an immortal lustre." John is silent. He tries to turn the conversation into other channels. It is easy for non-combatants to talk in that way in comfortable drawing-rooms, but war wears a different aspect in the trenches and on the battle-field. After the vicar has gone Mrs. Wharton, John's mother, again brings the conversation back to religion, and asks John if he will not attend the Communion Service next day—the last opportunity before his marriage. John tries to parry the question, but his mother presses him. Will he not do it for her sake ? John feels that he can no longer avoid the issue, so he replies that he can no longer take Communion. His mother is sorely troubled, and asks : " Do you mean to say that you've lost your faith ? " And John confesses that he has. His answer causes something like consternation. Both mother and father,

as well as his fiancée, press him with questions, and
Sylvia ultimately asks him : " Don't you want to believe
in God, John ? " And John answers, " No." The
conversation turns on the subject of Prayer and Death.
To Colonel and Mrs. Wharton, and also to Sylvia,
Prayer is a great spiritual resource. It must be such
an aid to courage, says his mother, to feel that one has
the Almighty to fall back upon in time of danger. " We
tried to bring you up to fear God," says Mrs. Wharton.
" It used to make me happy sometimes to see how simple
and touching your faith was. You used to pray to God
for all sorts of things." But John's experiences in the
war háve shown him the futility of that sort of prayer.
He has seen men, believing men, men full of the spirit
of prayer, killed, blown to pieces, and he has seen
profane, unbelieving men, men who never offered a
prayer since their childhood's days, escape. He knows
that thousands, millions of mothers, sisters, sweethearts,
children, have prayed that their dear ones might escape
death on the battle-field, but to no purpose. In such
things one might as well pray for bullets to be turned
into butter as pray for them to be miraculously deflected
from their billets. No, if we don't want our dear ones
to die on the battle-field we have got to make battle-
fields impossible—that is all. As for courage, prayer
and religious belief seem to make little or no difference.
Prayerful men showed great courage, men who never
prayed showed the same. But before one goes into
a hell of bullets, liquid fire, and poison gas, says John,
everyone who is not an imbecile feels a certain amount

of fear, and takes the necessary precautions. His father, the Colonel, observes towards the end of the conversation that " the Christian doesn't fear death. His whole life is but a preparation for that awful moment. To him it is a shining gateway to life everlasting." Yet, before an hour passes, the Colonel himself has received sentence of death, and is crying like a child to his wife that he does not want to die. For, during this scene, Dr. Macfarlane, the family doctor, has come in with a letter from a London physician whom Colonel Wharton had found it necessary to consult, and his report is that Colonel Wharton's heart is in such a serious condition that he may die any day.

There the first act ends. In the second act, which takes place after an interval of two days, these religious difficulties present themselves anew. Colonel Wharton has become worse. Everybody feels that Death is hovering over the house. The vicar, the Rev. Norman Poole, again calls, and has a long argument with John. He admits that every Christian " must have asked himself why God allows the infamous horrors of war. I'm told," he says, " that the padres are constantly being asked by the brave lads at the front why the Almighty allows it to continue. I can't blame anyone for being puzzled. I've wrestled with the question long and anxiously." And the only conclusion he can come to is that " the word ' Almighty ' does not mean powerful over all things." John objects that the distinction means nothing. " Either God can't stop the war if He wants to, or He can stop it and won't "—in which case the religious difficulty remains. In the midst of the discussion a Mrs. Littlewood, a neighbour, comes in. She has lost two sons in the war. On the death of the first she resigned herself to the blow as a sacrifice she must bear for her country. But God would surely never take her beloved younger son, the only joy left to her! But the younger son is killed also. As a result she loses not only her faith, but her interest in life. She listens to the discussion, however, but when the vicar begins to expatiate on the sinfulness of man, and says that God is ever willing to forgive men their sins, she electrifies the company by asking in a quiet voice: " And who is going to forgive God ? "

The vicar turns to her, and tells her she is talking blasphemy, but she replies :

" Ever since I was a child I've served God with all my might, and with all my heart, and with all my soul. I've tried always to lead my life in accordance with His will. I never forgot that I was as nothing in His sight. I've been weak and sinful, but I've tried to do my duty. . . . Honestly I've done everything I could that I thought was pleasing in His sight. I've praised Him and magnified His name. You've heard that my husband deserted me when I'd borne him two children, and I was left alone. I brought them up to be honest, upright, and God-fearing men. When God took my eldest son I wept, but I turned to the Lord and said : ' Thy will be done.' He was a soldier, and he took his chance, and he died in a good cause. . . . But why did God take my second ? He was the only one I had left, the only comfort of my old age, my only joy, the only thing I had to prevent me from seeing that my life had been wasted and it would have been better if I had never been born. I haven't deserved that. When a horse has served me long and faithfully till he's too old to work I have the right to send him to the knacker's yard, but I don't, I put him out to grass. I wouldn't treat a dog as my Father has treated me. I've been cheated. You say that God will forgive us our sins, but who is going to forgive God? Not I. Never. Never!"

In a frenzy of grief she rushes from the room. How many thousands, during the war, passed through the same experience!

The conversation is resumed, and when John asks the vicar the question which poses all theologians: " Why is evil permitted in the world by an all-good and all-powerful God?" the vicar can only reply: " By God's grace I am a Christian. You are an atheist " —which is simply untrue. Obviously, what John does not believe in is the miracle-working God of the vicar's creed. " By God's grace " forsooth! Why should the grace of God make one man a Christian and another an atheist?

But John has reckoned without his host. Sylvia, his fiancée, now joins in the conversation. She and John have been engaged to each other seven years, but she now says that she cannot marry an unbeliever.

John stands aghast, and exclaims: " Sylvia, Sylvia, you cannot mean that!" But Sylvia does mean it. John has come back from the war a different man. He went away a Christian, a believer. He has come back an Agnostic, an unbeliever. He is no longer the same John to whom she pledged her troth. She no longer trusts him. The God who is a living presence

H

to her, for John, does not exist. To Sylvia that is sin.
God has given him the choice between light and darkness, and he has chosen darkness, she says. If they
have children, she continues, and she teaches them to
pray at their mother's knee, is he, their father, going to
tell them that their faith and their belief are " a pack
of worthless lies ? " To John's appeal for charity and
tolerance, and a recognition of the fact that truth appears
in different ways to different minds she turns a deaf
ear. She takes her engagement-ring from her hand
and returns it to him, and the second act ends with the
disturbing incident that Colonel Wharton, John's father,
overcome by these heated discussions and agitating scenes,
has a sudden seizure and has had to be carried out of
the room.

A week elapses between the second and third acts.
It is early morning. John has gone out for a walk, and
while he is out his father, with whom Mrs. Wharton
has been sitting all night, dies. While John is away,
not knowing of his father's death, Sylvia, who still
remains on friendly terms with the family, comes in.
Mrs. Wharton begins to tell her of her husband's last
hours and how he has entered into eternal life. Almost
up to the last, she says, he had been afraid to die, and
then, when the vicar administered the Holy Sacrament
to him, a miracle happened.

" No sooner," says Mrs. Wharton, " had the bread
and wine touched his lips than he was transfigured. His
fear and anxiety left him. He was quite happy to die.
It was as though an unseen hand had pulled back a

dark curtain of clouds, and he saw before him, not night and a black coldness, but a path of golden sunshine that led straight to the arms of God."

"Yes, indeed," Sylvia echoes. "And if the Holy Sacrament can give such faith to the father's heart and drive all fear away," she says to herself, "why should it not change the heart of the son, and another miracle happen ? "

At that moment John returns from his walk while the mother has been called away. Sylvia does not tell him his father is dead. In fact, she deceives him. She leads him to believe that his father is still living, but near to death ; that he is anxious that his son should attend Holy Communion and take the Sacrament. The mother, too, she says, is anxious. She, Sylvia herself, is heart-broken. The bell is already ringing in the church calling the villagers to early communion. Will he not go and take the Sacrament ? Then his father will die in peace. His mother's life will be gladdened. And she, Sylvia, will take him to her heart again, and they will all be reunited in love and peace once more.

"For God's sake," she says, "go. Your father is dying ; the church bell is ringing. How can you be so hard ? Oh, John, it's your last chance of showing your love to your father. Have mercy on his weakness."

In the weakness of the moment John gives way. He goes down to the church, and receives Holy Communion. But he feels all the time that the thing is horrible, insincere, a lie in the very House of God. He is humiliated, and he goes back home feeling ashamed of his weakness, and as though he had become tainted with untruth in the soul. When he gets back he learns the truth. Sylvia confesses. She had expected a miracle, and the miracle has not happened. John feels that the lie has killed his love for her, and they are driven farther apart than ever as they realize the spiritual gulf which divides them. Sylvia prays to God to forgive her her sin, and the play ends with the matter-of-fact entry of the cook coming to inquire what she shall prepare for dinner.

The Unknown is not a great play. There is nothing of the genius of Shakespeare, of Ibsen, or of our great dramatists about it. But it is a striking and an interesting play, and it holds up the mirror to what has been going on in the minds of thousands of people during the past ten or twelve years. It helps to bring home to men the spiritual bankruptcy of much of our modern theology, and especially of the artificiality of the creeds. John Wharton rightly protests that he is not an atheist, but his terrible experiences on the battle-field have shown him that the conception of God which is taught in the earlier parts of the Bible and in the creeds is entirely out of accord with the facts of life—a God, as William Watson says :

> " A God like some imperious King,
>   Wroth, were His realm not duly awed,
> A God for ever hearkening
>   Unto His self-commanded laud,
> A God for ever jealous grown
> Of carven wood and graven stone.

> " O streaming worlds, O crowded sky,
>   O life, and mine own soul's abyss,
> Myself am scarce so small that I
>   Should bow to Deity like this !
> This my begetter ? This was what
> Man in his violent youth begot,"

—a God whose laws can be changed or suspended at the request of His worshippers, who will turn bullets aside, make bombs innocuous, bestow His favour or protection on this or that section of His children, and neglect the prayers of others, and when His worshippers have defied all the laws of health and sanitation will banish typhoid, malaria, plague, and other diseases by the magic of His will !

But though John Wharton, by the education of terrible experience, has seen the inadequacy and the falsity of this conception of God, he has not yet attained to a higher conception. The terrible cruelties, sufferings, and evils of the universe, especially as seen on the battle-field, where " but to think is to be full of sorrow," oppress him, as they oppress every thoughtful mind, and he cannot reconcile them—no man can reconcile them— with the theory of an all-powerful and all-loving God. The evils of war may, indeed, be accounted for by the ignorance, the follies, the ambitions, and the selfishness of men in the exercise of their free will, but these excuses cannot be offered for the evils of the earthquake, the pestilence, the famine, and the shipwreck. Surely, it would be better if our theologians would admit this difficulty fully and frankly instead of fencing with it

and teaching that if we will only pray with faith and
perseverance God will miraculously grant our desires
and petitions. No. Our desires and petitions cannot
be granted when they are contrary to the spiritual laws
of the universe. One might as well pray for water to
boil at 32 degrees and freeze at 212. Prayer, or the
answer to prayer, can only come in a spiritual way,
through and by means of our own minds and hearts,
our thoughts, our feelings, and through our thoughts
and feelings, our knowledge and our will. *Through us*,
not by arbitrary almightiness, the spiritual power of the
universe works. The object of true prayer is not to
change the mind or the Spirit of the universe, but to
bring our minds into the knowledge of and harmony
with that larger mind. Prayer, like aspiration and desire,
is a spiritual activity functioning in the spiritual sphere
of mind and heart, and such functioning is limited and
conditioned by the laws which govern the activities and
the development of the mind. Everyone will admit
that behind visible Nature, behind the vast phenomena
of the universe, behind oceans, stars, and planetary
systems, there is a mighty spiritual force at work which
seems to be struggling and agonizing towards the creation
of a better world. It does indeed produce the earthquake, the lightning, the shipwreck, the drought, and
consequent famine, but it produces also health and
beauty and the conditions which give to us our human
loves and joys—all that makes life worth the living.
Surely it is better to stress this aspect of the Spirit—
its agonizing struggles after something higher and better,

rather than its supposed Almightiness, and the declarations of impossible creeds, which have been deduced from this apparently illegitimate premise. For the highest, the most beautiful, the most permanent, and therefore, in the long run, the most powerful spiritual force in the universe is this Spirit of Love whose aim and purpose seems to be to triumph over ugliness, selfishness, cruelty, and wrong. In throwing all our thinking, our feeling, and our endeavours on the side of that Spirit we cannot go far wrong, for where the Spirit of Love is, there God, the highest spiritual power in the universe, is also. And that seems to be the conclusion to which Mr. Maugham, the author of this play, has come, for he puts into the mouth of the doctor of the village, who says he has never been to church for thirty years because he found he got no spiritual good from its services——he puts into the mouth of Dr. Macfarlane these words. He is speaking to Mrs. Littlewood, the lady who has lost her two sons in the war :

" I want to tell you, Mrs. Littlewood, how *I* found peace. My explanation is as old as the hills, and I believe many perfectly virtuous persons have been frizzled alive for accepting it. Our good vicar would say I was a heretic. I can't help it. I can't see any other way of reconciling the goodness of God with the existence of evil. . . . I don't believe that God is all-powerful and all-knowing. But I think He struggles against evil as we do. I don't believe He means to chasten us by suffering or to purify us by pain. I believe pain and suffering are evil, and that He hates them, and would crush them if He could. And I believe that in this age-long struggle between God and evil we can help, all of us, even the meanest ; for in some way, I don't know how, I believe that all our goodness adds to the strength of God, and perhaps—who can tell ?—will give Him such power that at last He will be able utterly to destroy evil—utterly, with its pain and suffering."

That is the creed of thousands of good men and women, and though it may not be infallible or even strictly logical at all points—and what human creed can be infallible ?—it is more in accord with the facts of life as modern science and knowledge unfold them, than the ancient creeds of our forefathers. Shelley was expelled from Oxford University for sucn heresies as those of John Wharton and Dr. Macfarlane, and yet Shelley, whose spirit lives to-day while the very names of his detractors are forgotten—Shelley was so filled with ethical and religious passion and emotion that he could write of the Spirit whom he worshipped those haunting lines :

" The awful shadow of some unseen Power
    Floats, though unseen, among us ; visiting
    This various world with as inconstant wing
As summer winds that creep from flower to flower ;
Like moonbeams that behind some piny mountain
        shower,
    It visits with inconstant glance
    Each human heart and countenance ;
Like hues and harmonies of evening,
    Like clouds in starlight widely spread,
    Like memory of music fled,
    Like aught that for its grace may be
Dear, and yet dearer for its mystery.

" Spirit of Beauty, that dost consecrate
    With thine own hues all thou dost shine upon
    Of human thought or form . . .
Thy light alone, like mist o'er mountains driven,
    Or music by the night-wind sent
    Through strings of some still instrument,
    Or moonlight on a midnight stream,
Gives grace and truth to life's unquiet dream."

Those lines are as impressive as any of the Psalms,
and the Church that cannot accept them as the out-
pouring of a deeply religious spirit has surely had
its day.

IV

SUTTON VANE'S *OUTWARD BOUND*.
THE OTHER SIDE OF DEATH.

Outward Bound is an interesting and thought-provoking
play ; interesting and thought-provoking because it deals
with a subject which is of universal interest. It is a
subject which is, perhaps, of greater interest to those
who are getting on in years than to those who have the
greater part of life before them. To youth, death appears
so far away that it has not the same compelling interest
that it has for those who are nearing Nature's bound.
Still, it is an experience through which we all have to
pass, and even light-hearted youth cannot escape the
solemn monitions and reminders of the time when man
goeth to his long home. This universal interest and
appeal makes the spectator feel as though he were part
of the drama, for in every one of the characters he sees
himself, or some of his friends, represented. In every

scene, in every dialogue, he is brought face to face with a moral situation, a moral problem, which has been presented to himself in his own experience of life. It was Ibsen who first vividly presented this new type of drama to the modern world—though similar situations arise in the ancient Greek drama—the drama, that is, which makes the spectator an unconscious partner in the play, which forces upon him certain questions which disturb and trouble his mind, heart, and conscience, and which, by its appeal to the intellectual side of his nature, lifts the drama out of the realm of mere sensationalism, sentimentalism, and false romanticism. I will show you, said Ibsen, the real meaning of the problems of life —the problem of heredity, the problem of religion, the problem of sacrifice, the problems of idealism and self-realization, and the struggles of the human soul with hypocritical conventionalism, snobbery, selfishness, in-sincerity, humbug, and political jobbery. I will show you these as they work out in your actual workaday lives, and homes, and city councils, and Parliaments, and Churches, and I will show you them in such a way that as you watch the play, you yourself, like the King in *Hamlet*, shall see yourselves as part of the drama, and be forced to ask yourselves the heart-searching and thought-provoking questions which may determine your conduct in life. And all this without preaching, without moral tags, without any sloppy sentimentalism, but by the sheer natural appeal or pressure of a moral situation which, as in a glass, is held up before our eyes.

In that respect *Outward Bound* is true to the modern

movement in drama, though it lacks the dramatic force, intensity, and power of characterization of the great masters.

For the benefit of those of my readers who have not seen or read the play let me briefly outline its story and *motif*.

The first act opens on board the steamer *Outward Bound*. A good deal is left to the imagination. There are only seven or eight passengers, who are received on board by the steward " Scrubby." These passengers are, briefly, a young man named Prior, who has gone to the bad and taken to drink ; a selfish society-woman named Mrs. Clevedon-Banks ; an egotistic and self-made merchant and speculator, Mr. Lingley of Lingley, Ltd. ; a good-natured London charwoman, Mrs. Midgett, given to gossip ; the Rev. William Duke, a clergyman, depressed at the failure of his work and out of a job ; a young couple who, in despair, are disposed to suicide ; and another clergyman, the Rev. Frank Thomson, who takes the part of Supreme Judge or Examiner.

Shortly after leaving port, the passengers begin to discover that there is something strange and eerie both about themselves and about the ship. There is no captain, no crew, only the steward Scrubby, and not one of the passengers seems to remember to what port the vessel is bound. In their intercourse with each other they have all manifested their natural personal habits and characteristics—their drinking or smoking habits, their selfishness, their egotism, their garrulousness ; in a word, their human frailties and shortcomings, and their kindly human interest in each other. The real truth is discovered by young Prior, the dipsomaniac. When he mentions it to his fellow-voyagers, they think he is mad or drunk. But the truth gradually dawns on all alike—they are doomed souls, on a phantom ship, sailing over an unknown ocean, voyaging to a land on the other side of death—heaven, hell, purgatory, the Elysian fields, the land of Shades, as the imagination or the theological bias of the spectator may determine. They call Scrubby, the steward, and he confirms their fears. They must prepare to meet the great Examiner—the Judge of all their lives! But Scrubby cheers their drooping spirits with the reminder that the land to which they are going is both Heaven and Hell in one—a variant of Omar Khayyám's well-known saying : " I myself am Heaven and Hell."

What is to be done ? They hold a meeting, at which Lingley, the business man, votes himself to the chair. *He* has nothing to fear ! Has he not made a success in life and climbed his way to wealth, position, and power ! Mrs. Clevedon-Banks, the heartless society woman, with her cruel tongue, is also unrepentant, and comes to the meeting suitably dressed, as she thinks, for the occasion. But the others are not so sure of themselves. They ask the clergyman, the Rev. Mr. Duke, to pray for them. But he declines. If, he says, there is one thing he has learnt in his ministerial life it is this : that no man is fit to pray for the forgiveness of another's sins—let him first purify himself of his own sins. Reproached, however, by Mrs. Midgett, the charwoman, for neglecting his duties, he repeats the simple childish prayer which he has learnt at his mother's knee, and the second act ends as the ship nears its destination, and the doomed passengers prepare to meet the great Judge.

But the great Judge, or Examiner, is not a very formidable being after all. He appears in the play as a human being, very much like ourselves—a hearty, rollicking, matter-of-fact clergyman with a sense of humour as well as a sense of justice, the Rev. Frank Thomson. The passengers appear in due order before him one by one. Lingley, the company-promoter, true to the commercial code of morality by which he has won success, lies and equivocates in the very face of the Examiner, and is soon sent packing to his doom. Mrs. Clevedon-Banks, the Becky Sharp of the piece, has her heartless selfishness exposed and held up before her eyes, and is sent to find retribution and purificatory experience with the husband to whom she was so cruel and unfaithful in her life on earth. But the flotsam and jetsam of life—those who have failed through weakness or temptation rather than through selfishness or malicious intent—to these a different fate is meted out. The half-forgotten, half-conscious impulses towards good, " the little unremembered acts of kindness and of love," the daily drudgery which seems to count for so little each day, but, in the end, helps in the building-up of spiritual life and personality—these are given an opportunity of developing into more fruitful service in other surroundings. Young Prior, the drunkard, who has been filled with remorse and despair, is granted another chance, but he is given to understand that the struggle will be one which will require all his inner resources of moral strength and will. Mrs. Midgett, the charwoman, who turns out to be the mother of Prior, finds her Heaven in being restored to her son, and in being given a little cottage in the country where she can nurse him back into health and sanity of life. And the young clergyman is given a field of labour in which his work shall not be entirely frustrate or useless. The only passengers who are not judged are the Half-ways, as they are called, the two lovers who, in their despair, had committed suicide, and who would not face with courage the difficulties in which they had found themselves. They must go back to earth. Indeed, the author of the drama leads us to suppose that the fumes of gas by which they had sought death had not taken their full effect. In any case they are sent back to earth to learn the lesson of life once more, and the play ends as the darkening night falls on the ghostly vessel and the unknown sea, to remind the spectators of the drama that our lives too are surrounded by the dim lights and shrouded veils of Eternity as we voyage over the mysterious ocean of life.

The play is an interesting one, but it lacks the note and the quality of greatness. If the reader will turn to Plato's vision of the judgment of souls in the *Republic*, or to Dante's *Divine Comedy*, or to Shakespeare's *Hamlet* or *The Tempest*, or to Shelley's *Adonais*, or to Lilith's soliloquy in the last act of Bernard Shaw's *Back to Methuselah*, he will see at once what I mean. But *Outward Bound* certainly reflects something of the modern religious spirit at a higher level than one finds it in much modern theology. In the drama the rewards, the punishments, and the destiny of the soul are not made to depend on belief in this or that ecclesiastical creed, the observance of religious ceremonial, or membership of any particular Church, but on the simple question : What have you done ? What is your record ? How have you lived ? That is, it lifts the problem of the after-life above the creeds and ritual of the Churches, into the clear light of the Eternal as prefigured and expressed by the great prophets of the race, in such sayings as :

" What doth the Lord require of thee but to do justly, and to love mercy, and to walk humbly with thy God."

" Whatsoever a man soweth that shall he also reap."

" Inasmuch as ye did these things unto one of these My brethren, even these least, ye did them unto Me."

But the underlying assumptions of the dramatist with regard to the conditions of the after-life are another matter. Mr. Sutton Vane seems to assume, as many people assume nowadays, that the after-life will be simply a continuation of this, under very similar conditions and surrounded by similar personalities. Our spiritualistic friends tell us that we shall be able to get our whisky-and-soda and cigars (or the illusion of them) on the other side, just as young Prior in the play was able to get more than was good for him. But how these things are manufactured or what becomes of their refuse we have no very precise information. Mr. Dennis Bradley tells us that one of his spirit acquaintances has produced a formula for the cure of cancer and tuberculosis, but we are not told how it was chemically built up, or what becomes of it when it is resolved into its original elements. And would it not be much more to the purpose to tell us how tuberculosis and cancer can be prevented ?

But this assumption, that life on the other side of the Veil is very similar to life here, seems to me to be a very large and not quite justifiable assumption, for various reasons. First, that on the hypothesis of survival, we shall be without the fleshly body, without all that physical machinery which, through the avenues of sensation, has so largely helped to build up our earthly life. That will be in the grave—dust to dust. Now, whatever ghostly or tenuous form and substance takes the place of that fleshly body, the change must make a considerable difference to our ways and modes of life, that is, to our sensations and experiences on the other side. Second, I believe that Death, and the way to Death, which is usually through suffering, will be a great spiritual revealer, just as every fateful experience is a great revealer. After all, Death is a tremendous experience, even more tremendous than birth, and, released from the flesh and the fettering clogs of mortality, it is surely permissible to suppose that the spirit will be able to see more clearly into the spiritual nature and the spiritual *values* of things —see the littlenesses, the meannesses, the trivialities, the foolish jealousies, the absurd and ridiculous pride, the vain strivings after position, and pomp, and power, and wealth, which make up so large a part of our life here, and which are caused by a sort of blindness which attaches to the flesh. Even in this life, especially as we get older, we see that. We see how small such things are, and especially such things as personal, sectarian, and political bitterness, as we draw near to Nature's bound. We become more charitable. We make allowance. We recognize the true spiritual values of life, and we see the ridiculous futility and pretentiousness of much that we had thought good and even necessary. And we shall surely make *more* allowance, when, on the other side, our spiritual sight pierces through to the *real* things, apart from the fleshly casement, and sees the wondrous working of the spiritual laws of heredity, and environment, and spiritual affinity, and the secret gravitation of those physical and spiritual forces which have impelled the soul this way or that. I do not say, indeed, how can one say—for we must all speak with hesitation and with a reverent agnosticism about things of which we know so little—how can we say to what extent our mind or spiritual nature will be changed ? Perhaps not essentially or fundamentally changed. The old desires, the old passions—modified, perhaps, by the change in methods of sensation—the old affections, the old spiritual aspirations and ideals, good or bad, may be still within us, waiting for further purification and development, but the experiences of suffering and death, and the added spiritual insight which such experiences bring, will surely give a larger meaning and a wiser power of spiritual direction to the developing soul. The old legend of Sisyphus, the wicked King of Corinth, is surely not a type of spiritual evolution. Even Dante's " Inferno," however high its value as poetry, is not a picture which we can accept in these days as that of a just or divine

I

dispensation. Punishment, to be just, must be remedial, purificatory, educative—" the medicine of the soul " as Plato calls it—not endless. Education and purification by experience mean, even here, deeper spiritual insight to direct the powers and faculties of the soul aright. And the spiritual laws which prevail here may surely be expected to prevail elsewhere.

There are two other points in which this drama seems to me to fail to drive home the eternal truths of life— two points which may be difficult to illustrate in drama, but which are certainly finely illustrated and emphasized by the greater dramatists, and also by other forms of Art. The first is this—that we are apt to take too small, too personal, and too selfish a view of what we may call the Life Beyond. All the passengers in *Outward Bound* are very much interested in *themselves*—they do not seem much interested in life *as a whole*. Now, in all great Art this conception of Life as a Whole—whether in the sphere of Beauty, of Truth, or of Good, is a moving, an inspiring, and a dominating conception. The great artist may not know, nay, being finite, he cannot know, the meaning of the Whole. But the urge of the Infinite is ever within him, the hand of the Eternal is ever upon him. Let me explain what I mean by a reference to evolution.

In primeval ages, before life appeared on the earth, the elements and atoms of which the earth was composed, in their ceaseless urge, movement, strife, combination, and recombination, were all preparing the world for a *Life Beyond their time*—the life of the ages and generations to come. In the next great age, when life appeared on the earth in the shape of the great flora and vegetable growths, that dim inchoate life was struggling, though not consciously, to prepare the world again as a habitation for a Life Beyond—the life of the fauna, the huge vertebrates and the invertebrates which were still to come. In the next great age, when animal life appeared on the earth in all its abundant and gigantic variety, that life was again preparing for a Life Beyond—the life of the anthropoids, the coming humanity. In the next great age, when the pre-human and the sub-human appeared, those sub-human and primeval races, as they roamed the primitive forests and settled in their lake-dwellings and cavern homes, were unconsciously preparing, in their turn, for a Life Beyond—the life of the coming civilized humanity as we know it to-day. So, too, with the great ancient civilizations—they were preparing for the next evolving stage of humanity. And in every stage of this unfolding and developing life we may be sure that the greatest, the most valuable, the most quickening and vitalizing elements or units would be those which gave themselves most generously and whole-heartedly to the making of the Life Beyond their life.[1]

"Ah, but," the reader may say, "in that case the Life Beyond meant some other life than their own— the life of a future humanity of which they could know nothing." That is true. But still, the idea is there—

[1] This idea is presented in greater detail in Mr. F. J. Gould's interesting little book, *Common-Sense Thoughts on a Life Beyond.*

the idea of a continuous life of the whole,[1] of which we are all part, vibrating in and through all, from earliest unknown ages, and worlds without end. Pascal was so impressed by this idea that he said that the whole history and life of humanity, " the whole succession of men during the ages, should be considered as One Man or One Being, ever living and constantly learning." For One Life, One Spirit, seems to pulse and surge through all—blindly and unconsciously through the inorganic realms, consciously through the organic, instinctively and intelligently through the vertebrates, affectionally and intellectually, and with a certain measure of spiritual discernment, through the higher ranges of human life, until it attains the vision of the One Life in which we are all units, necessary to each other, just as each individual but microscopic cell in our blood, bones, and body, helps to make up our individual life, having its daily work to do in the building up of that life, and without which unity of endeavour and co-operation we could not live. It is a thing of constant wonder to me, and it should be a thing of constant wonder to all of us, that we should not be living now, the reader would not be sitting reading this book now, but for all the millions of generations which have gone before, and all the mighty forces which have helped to build up this earth, and the universe, and human settlements and civilizations, all preparing for and converging into

[1] General Smuts emphasizes and makes use of the same truth in his *Holism and Evolution*. It is, of course, an essential part of idealistic evolutionary philosophy.

these little points of life as we are living them now. That is, we are parts, more than parts, we are co-workers in one continuous stream of life, one mighty and continuous stream of Being.

Now my point is this : that unless we keep and hold a high and vivid conception of this Life above and Beyond our life, this one-ness and solidarity of all life—which includes, of course, our own—and unless we can keep before our minds the necessity of living *for* that *One* life, giving up much of our little self that we may the more effectively live for the One—losing our little lesser self in order that we may gain a larger and more effective self ; unless we can do that, then our conception of the after-life or of immortality will be poor and thin, as that of many Christians is poor and thin—the tedium of a psalm-singing heaven or the horrors of a torture-driven hell. This element of spiritual greatness, of a greater and more expansive Life Beyond, I find in all great literature. I find it in the New Testament ; I find it in the great prophets, in Plato, in Dante, in Shakespeare, in Milton, in Wordsworth, in Shelley, in Ibsen, and in many others of our great poets and dramatists. I did not find it, at least not with the same sense of power and inevitability which belongs to great drama, in *Outward Bound*.

My second criticism is this. Has the reader ever considered how little of all that is most precious in life, in our own self or personality, is due to our own efforts, and how much is due to outside spiritual forces ? Take away, in imagination, all that has been given to us by our ancestry, by father and mother, by friends and companions, by education, by the mighty life of Nature, by Art and all the culture of the ages, the discoveries, the inventions, and the influence of the civilizations of the past—take all that away, and how much would there be left of our individual *self* that is really due to our own efforts ? How much ! Say, rather, how little, how very little ! Very well—if our debt is so great, if we owe so much to the mighty life of the Whole, to the stream of Being which we call God, how, in the name of all that is sacred, can we repay what we owe ? Nearly all the passengers in *Outward Bound*, save Mrs. Midgett and the clergyman, were thinking too much of their own little self, of their own safety, their own individual salvation. What I miss in the drama is that impelling something which would have filled them all, actors and spectators alike, with a sense of their own insignificance, unless, at the same time, they were filled with a sense of something fine, something great, mighty, Eternal, to which they belonged, and to which all who possess it are impelled to devote their lives in a fervent passion of devotion and of love, so that, losing their little earthly lives, they may perchance gain a larger life—" the life which is life indeed." Great art, great drama, and great poetry do give us that—the artist losing himself in his vision of ideal Beauty, the scientific worker in his vision of ideal Truth, and we common folk in our vision of the ideal Good, to which we have to learn to devote our lives. That is, Art, Poetry, Drama, and Religion, must not be content with cultivating merely a genial tolerance and good nature, necessary as these are ; they must give also a sense of depth and largeness of conception, and a power of insight, comprehension, and clearness of direction to our mind and spiritual life.

A much more artistic treatment of the problem of the after-life by means of the drama is given by Mr. Laurence Housman in his little play *Possession : A Peep-Show in Paradise*. The scene is fixed in what Mr. Housman calls " The Everlasting Habitations," and the play describes a middle-class Victorian household as it survives in the shadowy realm of the Elysian fields. The characters are two maiden ladies, Julia and Martha Robinson ; a third sister, married, Laura James ; their mother, Susan Robinson ; their father, Thomas Robinson ; William James, the husband of Laura ; and Hannah, the family servant. The household in this land of Shades is just a replica of the earthly home which these gentle and ungentle spirits have so recently left. But the chief characteristic of the play is the delicate irony with which the dramatist depicts the spiritual atmosphere—supposed by most of them to be heaven—in which his characters live. The cultured gentleness, slightly tinged with patronage and snobbery, of Miss Julia ; the acid, fault-finding disposition of Laura (Mrs. James) ; the dog-like loyalty and fidelity of the old servant, Hannah ; the depressed and subdued sister, Martha ; the gentle and lovable but self-willed mother ; the weak and shifty Mr. James, who has deserted his wife after enduring her as long as he could ; the dandified father who, like Don Juan, prefers the liveliness of hell to the tedium of heaven. All these are drawn with a delicacy which is none the less fine and effective because it is mingled with both irony and gentle charity. But the ethical principle underlying the little drama is that which is the foundation of Mark Twain's fine spiritual romance, *Captain Stormfield's Visit to Heaven*. Everyone gets what he desires—a harp, a halo, a pair of wings—and soon finds that the satisfaction of such desires palls.

" Things don't seem real here," says Laura.

" *More* real, I should say," Julia responds. " We have them—as we wish them to be." Except with persons. " We all belong to ourselves now. That one has to expect."

That is, the highest of possessions is self-possession. But how if the self we possess is a poor, attenuated, little, shallow self, which is cursed with an incurable blindness ? Here, we are back at the old problem of determinism, and I am afraid that Mr. Housman does not help us to solve it. For if we do but continue in the next life the self we have developed here, with all its shortcomings and blindness, who is responsible for that narrowing and encircling rim which determines the quality of the self ? Surely there must be some way out—perhaps through the purification of the spirit by sorrow and suffering—to greater light. Mr. Housman, I say, does not help us to answer these questions, but he does bring before us, much more subtly and artistically than does Mr. Sutton Vane, the psychological law which lies at the back of religion and spiritual evolution. The play ends in a futile and miserable little quarrel between the sisters about the " possession " of a silver tea-pot which Laura is anxious to get hold of, and which culminates in the following little dialogue :

LAURA.—" What is this place we've come to ? "
JULIA (*persuasively*).—" Our home."
LAURA.—" I think we are in hell ! "
JULIA.—" We are all where we wish to be, Laura." (*Exit ; leaving Laura in undisputed possession of the situation she has made for herself.*)

Exactly. " I myself am Heaven and Hell."

But quotation is useless in a play of this type. It is the atmosphere which the characters create by their various temperaments which tells upon the audience and the reader, and in the creation of this atmosphere Mr. Laurence Housman is an artist.

The treatment of the subject of the after-life in drama is very difficult, and I have no desire to be hypercritical. Both *Outward Bound* and *Possession* do help to give to the spectator a higher sense of spiritual values. When I compare Mrs. Midgett with Mrs. Clevedon-Banks, or with Mr. Lingley of Lingley Ltd., I cannot help thinking of the widow who cast her two mites into the Temple treasury, and of the thousands of youths who died on the battle-fields of Europe and Asia Minor longing for the cup of cold water, or offering such consolation as they could to a dying comrade. And yet we go on giving honours to our Midases and our Becky Sharps, to our Mr. Lingleys and Mrs. Clevedon-Bankses, and look upon them as the pillars of the State, the upholders of our Churches, the benefactors of our charities, and the cynosures of society. Both *Outward Bound* and

Possession are a rebuke to such false values and false judgments. In this respect they are a sign of the times. They show that many people, dissatisfied with the old conceptions of the Life Beyond, are seeking for new and more spiritual conceptions. For this belief in the survival and spiritual evolution of the soul is one of the most indestructible beliefs in the human mind. Even Huxley, agnostic though he was, confessed that he shrank from the thought of annihilation. To Browning the denial of the possibility of survival seemed to turn life into " a cheat and an imposture." And Mrs. Browning voiced the feelings of thousands of thoughtful minds in her poem *The Cry of the Human* :

> " ' There is no God,' the foolish saith,
>   But none, ' There is no sorrow ' ;
> And Nature oft, the cry of faith,
>   In bitter need will borrow.
> Eyes, which the preacher could not school,
>   By wayside graves are raised ;
> And lips say, ' God, be pitiful,'
>   Which ne'er said, ' God, be praised.'
>   Be pitiful, O God.

> *   *   *   *   *

> " We tremble by the harmless bed
>   Of one loved and departed ;
> Our tears drop on the lips that said
>   Last night, ' Be stronger-hearted.'
> O God, to clasp those fingers close,
>   And yet to feel so lonely !—
> To see a light upon such brows,
>   Which is the daylight only !
>   Be pitiful, O God."

It is this passionate longing of the human heart, and the craving for justice behind it—justice for the undeveloped or cruelly frustrate soul—which is at the root of the almost universal desire for survival ; the opportunity for the complete development of one's faculties and powers. " We should be slow to believe," says Dr. W. Macneile Dixon, in his thoughtful book on *Tragedy* :

" We should be slow to believe either that our logic and understandings carry us to conclusions concerning the mathematics and mechanics of the world wholly deceptive, or that nothing in it corresponds in any way to the structure and requirements of the soul, to that master passion, for example— putting aside for the moment all our other attachments and affections—for justice ; a passion which, if tragedy reveals anything, it discovers woven into the fabric of our being, and no more than logic in our power to surrender. ' I have within me,' wrote Euripides, ' within my soul, a great temple of Justice.' The tragic poets are no doubt in agreement that the Power behind the world has placed a heavy strain upon humanity and tried it far ; so far, indeed—since upon its dealings with us all turns—as to place deep in doubt its *principia*, whether of morals or of mind. Yet it were to think poorly, that is unpoetically, unimaginatively, of that Power as of majesty and strength *in excelsis*, the source of all that is, and at the same time as wholly senseless, or again as fair without and foul within, a heedless fountain of manifold and manifest injustices. The conclusion, though commonly enough entertained, strains comprehension, and appears to involve nothing less than the defeat of mind, a defeat it is not in the nature of poetry to acknowledge."

Neither is it in the nature of philosophy or religion to acknowledge such defeat. " The Kingdom of the

Spirit within," even though but in germ, leads us to look for, and to add our endeavours and our struggles to the realization of, the Kingdom of the Spirit without, not only here on earth, but, by the full bright exercise and unfolding of our best instincts, faculties, and powers here, to prepare them for full fruition elsewhere. It is this undying passion for Justice and Beauty in life which makes us feel " that we are greater than we know."

CHAPTER V

RELIGION AND THE DRAMA. CONCLUSION.

ERNEST RÉNAN is reported to have said that the last word in philosophy will come from the drama. Whether that be true or not there can be no doubt that the drama does bring into human consciousness flashes of truth which humanity will not willingly let die, and which help to give to human nature a clearer intellectual vision and a deeper spiritual insight. There are still many people who cannot agree with this, who cannot overcome their puritanical dislike of the theatre, or to whom play-acting is only as the dressing-up and imitativeness of the nursery carried on into the lives of grown-up children. The names of the great dramatists, from Æschylus, Sophocles, and Euripides, down to Shakespeare and our best modern playwrights, are a sufficient refutation of that point of view. But it is held, and will continue to be held, by large numbers of people in every generation, at any rate until art and parable, poetry and symbol, have taken their proper place in the education of our youth. For after all, the eternal mystery which surrounds our life must be approached in many ways : The way of Reason—science and philosophy ; the way of Art—picture, poetry, music, drama ; the way of Religion—symbol, ritual, chant, ceremonial. Indeed, until Religion learns to ally itself with Art and Philosophy, it will tend to go astray into the byways and intellectual mazes of theological narrowness and bigotry, or the lower deeps of magic and superstition.

We have seen in the foregoing chapters how the drama has helped, and may help still further, to free us from these narrow forms of religion. For the subject-matter of both Religion and the Drama, at its best, is the same —the conflict of the soul of man with himself, that is, with his hereditary tendencies, and with nature, environment, destiny, and all that these imply ; and the way of escape through suffering, endurance, penitence, spiritual insight, and reconciliation with the spiritual laws of the universe. We know how the Greek dramatists and Shakespeare dealt with these high themes. Or, to come to more modern instances, we remember how Ibsen threw the light of his genius on the problems of heredity and determinism. His *Emperor and Galilean* may be described as the drama of the conflict between Christianity and Paganism in the mind of Julian. Shaw's *Man and Superman* and *Back to Methuselah* are dramas of creative evolution—" a religion that has its intellectual roots in philosophy and science, just as mediæval Christianity has its intellectual roots in Aristotle " ; while Tolstoy's *The Light Shines in Darkness* is a drama of the application of the Sermon on the Mount to modern life. The riddle of life presents itself to the dramatist and the theologian alike, as it does to all of us, but while the theologian answers the riddle with a cut-and-dried scheme, the dramatist portrays its ever-varying influence on the human soul, and leaves the way open for further interpretations of its mystery. The mystery is too deep, the Infinite too vast, he virtually says, to be summed up in a formula. It can only be faced wisely and courageously by strong personalities ; these personalities the dramatist creates for us, and so, by his art, draws our sympathies towards them, and by so drawing them, unconsciously influences the development of our own spiritual nature and affinities. Who has not been moved by the irresolution and the temptations of a Hamlet or a Faust, or by the patient heroism of a Cordelia, an Imogen, or a Hermione ?

In one of the ablest reviews of my previous book, *The Ethical and Religious Value of the Drama*, the Reviewer,[1] in an acutely critical, but not unsympathetic, notice, said that " it is humanity, and not Nature, not the intellectual problem, that moves Mr. Balmforth." That is only partly true. It is a question of emphasis, and it may be that I tend to over-emphasize the human element. But in a book which began with the problem of *Job* and ended with Thomas Hardy's *The Dynasts*, one could hardly avoid seeing and stating the intellectual problem which besets us all. I refer to the matter here in order to point out that it is the human element in all drama which necessarily engages our attention and the attention of the dramatist. Nature is the background, the given thing, with which we have to make terms, perforce. It is the human element, therefore, in strife with Nature and circumstance, that must always move us and engage our attention most. As my Reviewer

[1] In *The Times Literary Supplement*.

himself said : " The sum of all these dramas and their like is that life involves itself in tragedy ; we strive and suffer, are seemingly defeated, and still aspire. Man is divided against himself and against his fellows. There is laughter and tears in discovering how far the individual and the race come short of their conceived ideals. And man is barely able to discern agreement between his own realm, the universe within, and the realm of Nature, the universe without. He is dismayed when he is constrained to set the outward fact, the whole environment, against the needs and desires of humanity. If the kingdom of man is contemplated, it is as if recourse must be had to mockery or pity. And if we search out the secrets of nature, the government of the universe, we are speedily brought to a stand by the impenetrable ; and such systems as we conceive, theological and scientific, tend to our distress. The human cry, from Job and Æschylus to Mr. Bernard Shaw and Mr. Hardy, is a cry for knowledge and justice."

That is true. And all our arguments become intellectual counters. We throw the ball to Nature and Nature tosses it back to man and man again to Nature, for

> " Nature is made better by no mean,
> But Nature makes that mean."

That is why the best dramatists cannot possibly be complacent or easy-going optimists. They see that life is never complete, and therefore that Art, which to the seeing mind is a reflection and a criticism of life, cannot be complete either. The last word cannot be

said. Hence their moods. Their main interest is the
unending struggle and conflict of man with Nature and
destiny. And in contemplating that struggle, who has
not his moods ? Shakespeare has his moods. He is
pessimistic in *Hamlet, Macbeth, Lear*, and *Timon* ; melioristic in his lighter plays and in the *Tempest*. Ibsen
sways between meliorism and pessimism, with a tendency
towards the latter—though his *Epilogue* gives one pause.
Goethe, Shelley, Tolstoy, Hauptmann, Shaw, and Galsworthy are melioristic. Barrie is optimistic, with an
undertone of sadness. Hardy is pityingly pessimistic ;
Strindberg and Pirandello harshly and bitterly so, though
the latter's pessimism is relieved by his humour. But
these classifications do not help us, save that they help
us to classify ourselves, which is something.

On the other hand, our theologians, by contrast, are
too often complacent and easy-going optimists. It is
their business to justify the ways of God and Nature
to man, but they seldom face the seamy side of the
problems of life frankly and boldly. They remind one
of a boy going along a lonely road or through a wood
in the dark, and who whistles to keep up his courage.
We have all, sometime, to pass through the dark forest,
and we must face that pass alone. Whistling, or the
patter of a creed, will not save us. But the alert, clear-
eyed stoicism of the dramatist will keep us ever prepared.
" If it be now, 'tis not to come ; if it be not to come,
it will be now ; if it be not now, yet it will come. The
readiness is all."

As a matter of fact, the dramatist teaches us what

K

the theologian seldom teaches us. The theologians—save a wise one here and there like Hooker, who bids us, on these high themes, let our words be few—the theologians, with their rather narrow dogmatism, their schemes and plans of salvation, and their carefully prepared creeds and ritual, fitted only to their own type of mind, have yet to learn that life, like the drama, is an art—the greatest of all the arts. We chatter about pictures and sunsets, and " we look at Nature too much and live with her too little," as Oscar Wilde said after he had eaten the bitter bread of suffering and sorrow. But when we have learned the art of life as Jesus of Nazareth learned and taught it, we shall try to live as simply and as beautifully as the flowers, with hearts like the innocent heart of a little child ; with the grace, the beauty, the simplicity, the serenity of Nature herself at her loveliest and best. It is the poet and the dramatist, rather than the theologian, who help us here, because they teach us to look upon life as an art.

But is it not possible to bring the theologian and the philosopher, the poet and the dramatist, into line with each other, so that, in their respective spheres of influence, they may work together against the dark forces of ignorance, materialism, and greed which at present menace our civilization ? The average thoughtful person, when he goes to the theatre, cannot but feel that he is in a much more tolerant atmosphere than in the church. He goes to the theatre with an open mind, and he is encouraged, almost unconsciously, to keep an open mind.

But when he goes into a church he feels, and he is made to feel, that he is expected to adopt a given point of view and to close his mind to other points of view. Indeed, in many of the churches, he will be told that if he does not accept the point of view—the creed and the ritual—which is being presented, he will be in danger of spiritual condemnation both in this world and the next. All our best dramatists, however, and all our greatest prophets and religious teachers, are utterly opposed to this narrowness and intolerance of spirit and temper. Indeed, if our colleges of science and philosophy were to adopt the exclusive and intolerant methods of many of the Churches, they would soon find themselves empty of students. Outside the Churches we have, at any rate, got thus far on the road of intellectual and spiritual advance—that the spirit of man will not brook any opposition to the freest intellectual inquiry, will not limit itself to a given theory, or consent to close its mind to any theory, either scientific or religious, without investigation. The best drama recognizes, and has always recognized this, and it almost unconsciously adopts this open-minded attitude as part of the natural order of things. Obviously then, if the Churches are to gain the influence which the best drama and the best theatres exercise, they must change their attitude and show a more tolerant intellectual spirit. The present crisis in the Church of England, and the conflict between Fundamentalism and Modernism in America, are portents of the struggle that is to come. No Church and no religion, especially in view of the work accomplished by the science of Comparative Religion, can henceforth assume an attitude of spiritual superiority to all the others and say : " Salvation lies with us—you are beyond the pale." Each must be judged by its spirit and its fruits. We want a League of Religions as well as a League of Nations, and the representatives of every religion must be willing to sit down at a common table in conference with each other, ready to compare notes with regard to the influence of any and all forms of religion on life, conduct, and the future development of humanity—nationally, racially, and as a whole. Here we are back at the spirit of " gentle persuasion " of Æschylus, the divine tenderness of the Second Isaiah, the Wisdom of Ecclesiastes, Ecclesiasticus, and the Greek thinkers, the " sweet reasonableness " and " method of inwardness " of Jesus of Nazareth, and the Spirit of " Mercy, Pity, Peace, and Love " of Blake, Wordsworth, Shelley, Keats, and others of our modern poets. The Churches themselves must make this spirit their own ere they can hope to dispel the black clouds which at present lour over civilization, by that combination of " sweetness and light," of wisdom and understanding love, which it is the aim of art, poetry, drama, and the highest kind of religion to instil.

And there is a meeting-point, many meeting-points, between the two—between religion and drama. The deeps of personality, the healthy pleasures of more abundant life, charity in our judgments, the relation of the individual to society, and of the soul to the higher spiritual powers—these are the subject-matter of both religion and the drama. " Fear, joy, grief, hope, pride, pity, patience, disgust, loyalty, fortitude, admiration, and all the rest," says Dr. W. Macneile Dixon, in his little book on *Tragedy* :

" . . . each affected by the group to which it belongs, influenced by the interest that for the moment rules, weave within the soul their eternal dance of an intricacy inconceivable, taking to themselves now one partner and now another, executing new steps and figures in ever-altering communities. Sorrow in company with anger, with envy or with apathy ; courage linked with hope or with despair ; wonder joined now with alarm, now with delight ; love with fear, with tenderness, or with ferocity ; pity hand in hand with sweetness or, again, with anguish — a bewildering spectacle, as of the motes in a sunbeam, tracing in their interminable, interlacing curves a plot beyond the possibility of the draughtsman, beyond any mathematical determination. For who will draw for us a stellar chart of our nature, in which inherited instincts organized in our bodily structure, actions reflex and reflective, habits, interests, purposes, desires, sentiments, affected in their several degrees by thoughts of self, sex, family, friends, religion, country—all the diverse emotional and intellectual promptings, are assigned each its exact place and influence in the Milky Way, the constellation of the soul ? "

Already one can discern in the thought of our best religious teachers—and not alone in Christianity—something of the spirit which will determine the growth and development of the future. In the emphasis, for example, which is being increasingly laid on the essential importance of personality—that each personality must be regarded as an end in itself, and that spiritual values must be judged and determined by their influence and effect on the development of personality. For

> " We are here as on a darkling plain,
>   Swept with confused alarms of struggle and flight,
>   Where ignorant armies clash by night."

In that struggle and flight, how supremely important is personality ! Here, the field of the dramatist is a wide one, and his great gallery of created personalities, from Prometheus to Hamlet, from Antigone to Cordelia, subtly and unconsciously moves us to admiration or repulsion, and, so moving us, moulds our own spiritual nature. The thought prolongs and extends itself and carries us into the field of ethics and religion. For if, as Matthew Arnold said, " the sympathy which is in human nature will not allow one member to be indifferent to the rest, or to have a perfect welfare independent of the rest "; and if " man is civilized only when the whole body of society comes to live with a life worthy to be called human, and corresponding to man's true aspirations and powers," then the question of personality becomes supremely important both for ourselves and for the future of society and civilization. We have to ask ourselves whether we can carry all our brothers with us towards this renovated society, this " kingdom of Heaven on earth "—the undeveloped and backward races, and the mentally and physically defective among our own peoples, or whether, in our selfishness and our blindness or lack of foresight, we have not allowed them to slip too far behind until they have become a menace and a danger, and how far a better environment or eugenic reforms can turn the current of human destiny, and influence deeply for good the physical and spiritual characteristics of the race. But these are questions which are of the very essence of the problems of ethics and religion, and make part of those " confused alarms of struggle and flight " which fill the thought of our time with apprehensions and forebodings, and

> " Shake our dispositions
> With thoughts beyond the reaches of our souls."

As Sir J. G. Frazer, in summing up his lifelong and profoundly interesting investigations into the history of religious customs and usages,[1] so truly and wisely says :

" The advance of knowledge is an infinite progression towards a goal that for ever recedes. We need not murmur at the endless pursuit. . . . Great things will come of that pursuit though we may not enjoy them. Brighter stars will rise on some voyager of the future—some great Ulysses of the realms of thought—than shine on us. But a dark shadow lies athwart the far end of this fair prospect. For however vast the increase of knowledge and of the power which the future may have in store for man, he can scarcely hope to stay the sweep of those great forces which seem to be making silently but relentlessly for the destruction of all this starry universe in which our earth swims as a speck or a mote. . . . Without dipping so far into the future, we may illustrate the course which thought has hitherto run by likening it to a web woven of three different threads—the black thread of magic, the red thread of religion, and the white thread of science. Could we then survey the web of thought from the beginning, we should probably perceive it to be at first

[1] *The Golden Bough.*

a chequer of black and white, a patchwork of true and false notions, hardly tinged as yet by the red thread of religion. But carry your eye farther along the fabric, and you will remark that, while the black and white chequer still runs through it, there rests on the middle portion of the web, where religion has entered most deeply into its texture, a dark crimson stain, which shades off insensibly into a lighter tint as the white thread of science is woven more and more into the tissue. To a web thus chequered and stained, thus shot with threads of diverse hues, but gradually changing colour the farther it is unrolled, the state of modern thought, with all its divergent aims and conflicting tendencies, may be compared. Will the great movement which for centuries has been slowly altering the complexion of thought be continued in the near future? Or will a reaction set in which may arrest progress, and even undo much that has been done? To keep up our parable, what will be the colour of the web which the Fates are now weaving on the humming loom of Time? Will it be white or red? We cannot tell. A faint glimmering light illumines the backward portion of the web. Clouds and thick darkness hide the other end."

That may be a depressing picture, but it is true to the teaching of history as we see it unrolled before our eyes. It is for us to illumine it with the lights and the pictures of drama, poetry, music, parable, and the best kind of religion, so that, by high Imagination,

> " which in truth,
> Is but another name for absolute power
> And clearest insight, amplitude of mind,
> And Reason in her most exalted mood,"

we may be beguiled out of our darkness, and so learn by these purer lights, to thread our way, even if it be only in idea as Plato says, towards the " plains of Heaven."

INDEX

INDEX

An Outline History of the Japanese Drama
By FRANK LOMBARD

Demy 8vo. *Illustrated* 16s.

This book is the outgrowth of interest developed through twenty-five years of teaching Shakespeare and the Western Drama in Japanese universities. It is not technical, nor in the narrow sense scholarly, but suggestive. Its chief introductory thesis is that the Japanese Drama is of social origin, and that the free expression of social dramatic instinct became repeatedly formalized by the patronage of organized religion, which alone was able to give it literary form and consequent permanence. This process is traced in the development of the *Kagura* and again in the development of the *Noh*. The third line of development was less impeded and led to the *Kabuki*, which is the more direct antecedent of the modern drama. Abundant material in translation is presented in illustration of the various dramatic forms, including early labour chants, *Kagura*, varied forms of *Noh*, a classic from Chikamatsu for the doll theatre, and a retold story from the relatively modern *Kabuki*.

Punch and Judy
With an Introduction by CHARLES HALL GRANDGENT, and Illustrations by GEORGE CRUIKSHANK

La. Cr. 8vo. *Illustrated* 3s. 6d.

The tragical comedy of Punch and Judy, as set forth in these pages, follows a version of the puppet-play more than a century old. It was taken down by George Cruikshank and Payne Collier, from a performance given in "a low-public house" by one Piccini, an elderly Italian and "a famous Performer of that popular Exhibition." It is thus a faithful record, made at a time when the art of puppet-playing was at its height; the text is extraordinarily droll, and Cruikshank's drawings capture the very spirit of Punch, Toby, Jack Ketch, the Devil, and "the nasty baby."

Shakespeare Music
Edited by E. W. NAYLOR, Mus.D.

Demy 4to. *Second Edition* 10s.

A collection of contemporary music intended to be useful in the production of the plays of the period and to convey sound instruction in the actual features of the music of the time. Included are some vocal pieces of the time of Henry VIII, intended to serve as an introduction to pre-Elizabethan music.